The Christmas Tag

The Christmas Tag

"Glorifying God's Name from Tragedy to Triumph"

Linda Atkins

Library of Congress Control Number: 2019901870
ISBN: Hardcover   978-1-7960-1624-6
              Softcover   978-1-7960-1623-9
              eBook   978-1-7960-1622-2

Scripture quotations marked NIV are taken from the Holy Bible, New International Version®. NIV®. Copyright © 1973, 1978, 1984 by International Bible Society. Used by permission of Zondervan. All rights reserved. [Biblica]

Any people depicted in stock imagery provided by Getty Images are models, and such images are being used for illustrative purposes only.
Certain stock imagery © Getty Images.

Print information available on the last page.

Rev. date: 02/14/2019

To order additional copies of this book, contact:
Xlibris
1-888-795-4274
www.Xlibris.com
Orders@Xlibris.com
791180

Contents

Preface

Starting off the new year in 1990, I began praying that the Lord would let others see Jesus through me. I am not one to strike up a conversation to share my faith with total strangers in the produce department as some of my friends do, so I wanted others to see Christ through the way I loved Him and lived my life. The Lord honored my request in a way I would never have chosen and caught me totally off guard as He called our youngest son home to Heaven.

As I share this story, it is my prayer that each reader will understand the importance of knowing Jesus as their personal Savior. Next, I pray that they will believe that God is trustworthy, has a plan for each of our lives, and will always keep our heads above water on the days we feel like we are drowning.

I want to thank our family, friends and even the strangers who cried and grieved with us, who listened to us pour our hearts out countless times, and remembered us with cards, calls, and gifts after Jeff's death. Each gesture was such an enormous part of our healing process, and you all were such a blessing. A special thank you to Joyce Dunavant who was my biggest encourager to write this book, and to all of you who have prayed for me as I took a deep breath and started reliving Jeff's life and death. Thank you, Dodie, for specifically praying for total recall – it worked. A debt of gratitude to Whitney Prosperi for the countless times she read my rough drafts and applied her editing skills and suggestions. "This is my story, this is my song, praising my Savior all the day long."

Linda Atkins

The Lord continued to meet our needs as the days and months sped by. We were now facing our second Christmas without Jeffrey. It was late one night, and I was wrapping packages and needed a certain color ribbon. I went to the bookcase where I kept bows and ribbons and found none. I wearily glanced at the next bookcase doors to my left. For some reason, I opened them and looked in. There was no ribbon, but tucked under a stack of papers with a corner sticking out, was a piece of faded green construction paper with cotton balls on it. I picked it up and found a Christmas card made by Jeffrey at an early age. Printed large and neatly was our message. *"Dear Family, Merry Christmas and Happy New Year, Love Jeff."*

The unusual thing wasn't that I kept the card all those years, because I kept all of Jamey's and Jeff's special school papers, but the fact that it was where it was and that I even looked there. Once again, I sat staring at yet another treasure I had found that let me know the

Lord was continuing to heal our broken hearts. I was grateful that the message this time wasn't just to me, but to our family. I again shared this in our Christmas letter to our family and friends.

Another year passed, and we were starting our third Christmas without Jeff. I was busy preparing for the holidays and for about a week and a half, I had a strong feeling I should go upstairs and look in his folders where he had kept his correspondence, but I didn't want to! I kept ignoring the urgings until finally I gave in. In the first folder I found two homemade cards. One was a Calvin and Hobbs drawing wishing everyone a Merry Christmas, and the other was the one we copied on red paper and used as our Christmas card that year. It was written in perfect calligraphy, and on the front it read: *"Remember the Reason for the Season."* Inside was written, *"for Jesus Christ was born on this day! Have a Merry Christmas!! Jeffrey Atkins."* Again, I was overwhelmed with gratitude and felt a little ashamed it had taken me so long to obey that inner prompting.

As the fourth Christmas approached, I had a friend keep calling to see if we had received our special message yet. I kept telling her no, I wasn't expecting one. I felt like the Lord had sent encouragement messages to me first, then to our family, and next to our friends, and that was enough. I knew the Lord could keep this up for many years, but we were fine, and I trusted He would continue to encourage us in other ways. He promises to never leave us or forsake us and to meet all our needs. He did then and still does today!

As you read this book, my prayer is that I will glorify the Lord and encourage you while sharing how the Lord carried our family through the most devastating time of our lives. May I challenge you to read God's Word and claim His promises. There may come a time in your life when this will be the only thing that will get you up in the mornings and carry you through the day. God's Word never changes, and His promises are true. There is a scripture in the Bible that states, "God's ear isn't so dull that He cannot hear, nor His arm so short that He cannot save." (Isaiah 59:1)

There were many days that I cried out for the Lord to hear my plea for help and pull me out of the pit of despair. He did time after time. I would visualize myself in the bottom of a deep pit, quoting that scripture, crying out to be rescued and sense His hand reach down and grasp mine, slowly pulling me up and setting my feet on solid ground again. May it be perfectly clear that what He did for us, He will do for you too, if you put your faith and trust in Him. As Christians, we aren't promised a life without heartache, trials, and tribulations, but we are promised peace amidst our storms.

"GLORIFYING HIS NAME FROM TRAGEDY TO TRIUMPH"
"I will give thanks to Thee, O Lord my God, with all my heart, and will glorify Thy name forever." Psalm 86:12

Chapter 1

Off to College

"Life is what happens when you're busy making plans" reads a sign given to me in March of 1990 by my brother-in-law's sister. She had received it when their daughter was killed in an accident years earlier. It has been hanging in my utility room ever since as a reminder that while we are busy making plans, they can change forever in the blink of an eye.

In the fall of 1989, Jerry and I followed our two sons, Jamey and Jeffrey, to Texas Tech University in Lubbock, Texas. Jamey, being three years older than Jeff and already a Red Raider, would live in an apartment and Jeffrey would be in a dorm. I sniffed and cried most of the long drive there, knowing that for the first time in many years, our house would be void of the constant in and out of kids, their many activities and the excitement from the presence of young people.

Both boys were graduates of Westfield High School, and Jeffrey was a senior in the fall of 1988 when Coach Emory Bellard, former coach at University of Texas, Texas A&M, and Mississippi State, came out of retirement to coach football at the high school level. Jeffrey wasn't a big kid, about 5' 10", weighing 155 lbs., but had always loved football. Jamey and his friends would let Jeff play ball with them down at the park, so he had learned at a very early age to stay tough with the big kids. Jeff played quarterback for the Mustangs and Jerry and I were on the Athletic Booster Club Board. We all had a wonderful, fun filled year, organizing get-togethers for the parents and players. Jeff got quite a bit of media coverage because of his position and, more importantly, because his coach was Emory Bellard.

We arrived in Lubbock safely and visited the local Sam's club store to buy the necessities the boys needed such as microwaves, groceries and even a radar detector for those long trips back home.

1

We got the boys settled in with Jeffrey meeting his roommate and other kids in the dorm and Jamey in his apartment with his friends.

Jerry and I spent the night at a hotel and met the boys for breakfast the next morning. Jeffrey came in first and we asked where Jamey was. He said, "Oh, he's in the middle of the street helping a man start his car. He'll come in soon." Jeff had told us more than once we should have named Jamey 9-1-1 because he never passed up anyone in need. After breakfast, we said our goodbyes, gave last minute instructions, and started back home. It was a long and mostly silent trip back, but I survived and quickly got busy with "life" once again.

We talked with the boys regularly, and they were happy and having a good time. Jamey reported that Jeffrey and his friends would arrive at his apartment on Sunday evenings in time for dinner since the dorm cafeteria was closed. Jamey's biggest concern was that the expense was coming out of his pocket, hinting for us to add more money to his account.

He also reported an incident that occurred when he was in the shower getting ready for a date. Jeffrey paid him a visit and discovered a new shirt laying out on the bed for Jamey to wear. As the story goes, Jeff put the new shirt on, leaving his old one in its place and escaping the scene of the crime before Jamey got out of the shower. I started to realize that nothing had changed with these two because Jeffrey had pulled that same trick while the boys were living at home. Jeffrey had always liked Jamey's clothes better than his if they were Polo shirts. However, Jamey was safe with his Wrangler jeans and western shirts which he mostly wore.

With the boys away at college and no more school activities to keep us busy, our neighbor Lori and I decided we would volunteer at Houston Northwest Medical Center. We signed up for two days a week: Monday mornings and Friday afternoons. I remember talking to Jamey one day, telling him of my new "adventure." About an hour later, I got a phone call from Jeffrey. He had to hear for himself that I was volunteering at a hospital. He could not believe it! It seems that I didn't have a very good reputation for being a compassionate nurse as I was one of those parents that assumed an injury wasn't as bad as the kids thought it was. Also, I certainly didn't like the sight of blood or needles. I assured Jeff that being a hospital volunteer had nothing to do with nursing, and that Lori and I thought being a volunteer would be fun and helpful.

Jeffrey started playing intramural football at Tech. I was told, after the fact, that on one occasion he was taken to the emergency room with a concussion. That was a big concern for us because the same thing had happened his senior year at Westfield and he had spent the night in the hospital. The doctor had told us previously that once you have a concussion, you are susceptible for more. Jeffrey had a wonderful time and made many new friends, but we were happy when his football season ended at Tech.

During Jeff's senior year in high school, he had started dating a young lady named Karen who was a grade behind him. His first trip home from Tech was to take her to the homecoming activities. He accidentally "forgot" to bring his suit for the dance on Saturday night, so he made a quick trip to Mr. Z's Men & Boys store in Town & Country shopping center for a new suit. This had been our "go to" store for special occasions since Jamey was in middle school because of their selections, superior fits and alterations. Jeffrey found the perfect suit, they rushed to alter it, and he came home with suit, shirt, and tie, ready for a fun evening.

The boys traveled home for the Thanksgiving holidays and back again for Christmas. Of course, they couldn't carpool because they would both need their cars to make the rounds to see their friends. Christmas was as busy as ever, and I remember trying my best to get a family photo while we were all together, but finally gave up since the boys were constantly in and out. I had to settle for separate snapshots, which I had no idea would become priceless treasures in a few short months.

We celebrated the holidays with Jerry's family at his mom's house. Jerry's dad had passed away the previous spring, so Christmas was different without him. After visiting his mom, we were off to my parents' farm in Jefferson, Texas. I have such sweet memories of this trip with a visual of Mother standing at the kitchen sink and Jeffrey next to her with his arm around her shoulders. They were looking out the window at the beautiful view and talking. It was this same trip that Jeff called me aside and said, "Did you see that? Granny D took Paw-Paw a cup of coffee, and he hadn't even asked for it! She is so nice!" This wasn't any new thing Mother did, but apparently it was the first time he had noticed, and he was extremely impressed.

With the holidays over and everyone settling in for a new year, the next time Jeffrey would come home would be to take Karen to the Valentine's Dance in February. This time, he remembered his suit and only had to buy a new tie. It was a quick trip where we saw very little of him, but we enjoyed having him home again.

Chapter 2

Devastating News

We were now into the month of March and all was well. The boys were anticipating Spring Break and Jeffrey had asked to fly home for Easter instead of driving. Jerry was working, and I was busy with Ladies Retreat reservations at church and my volunteer duties at Houston Northwest Medical Center.

On Sunday, March 4, Jerry and I went to Sunday school and church as usual. There we learned that a couple in our class had lost their twenty-two-year-old son in an automobile accident the night before. We did not know this couple well, but I was very burdened to hear this news. I prayed for them all week and grieved the loss of their son.

On Tuesday, March 6, my next-door neighbor, Lori, and I were taking our morning walk. I told her about the couple in our Sunday school class whose son had died and how sad I was for them. We stopped in front of the fire station in our neighborhood to discuss their loss. I told her I had asked the Lord to never take either one of my boys from me because I was certain I would not survive. We agreed how awful that would be, and somehow Lori started talking about how devastated she would be if anything ever happened to Jeffrey.

Lori has one son Brian, and we had lived next door to them since he and Jeff were turning four years old. She told me that Jeffrey was like a son to her, and she was certain she couldn't bear it if anything happened to him. She went on and on. We finished our walk, and when I got home I remember thinking, *That was the strangest conversation Lori and I have ever had. Why were we talking about something happening to Jeff?* I reflected over every detail of our conversation then dismissed it from my mind and went on about my day.

Making plans for his trips home, I talked to Jeff a couple of times that week. He was excited to report that a high school friend who was attending Texas A&M was coming to spend the weekend with him. We knew this young man and his parents well and were excited for the boys to reunite. This would be the final conversation I would ever have with Jeffrey. The last words he ever heard me say were, "I love you," and the last words I would ever hear him say were, "I love you too!"

Jamey was home, and he and I had gone to visit my parents in Jefferson for a couple of days. We came home Friday morning, March 9, so I could volunteer at the hospital that afternoon. Jerry and I went out to eat Friday night, March 9, 1990, and later went to bed after the ten o'clock news.

At 1:20 a.m. the phone rang loudly on my side of the bed. It was the call that all parents dread. Jeffrey's college roommate, James, called to tell us that Jeffrey had been in a terrible car accident. I asked him if Jeff was okay and he said, "No ma'am. He has a head injury and is in a coma." I asked whose car was involved and if anyone else was hurt. Unable to know what else to say, I told James I was going to hand the phone to Jerry so he could get the details.

The minute I handed Jerry the phone, it was like a choir of angels started singing a chorus we sang at church many times, "Glorify Thy Name," over and over in my head. This song would continue to consume my mind with calmness over the next two days.

Jerry attained the name of the hospital, necessary phone numbers and information regarding what had happened. The story we received was there were two carloads of Tech kids that had met for pizza and then went bowling. A severe rainstorm had hit Lubbock that night and there was still water in low places on the streets. They headed back to the dorm around midnight with a carload of friends taking one route and Jeff's car taking another. Jeff's friend from A&M was driving too fast and unexpectedly hit water and hydroplaned. This caused him to lose control, crashing into one car and spinning around into another one. Each time they hit a car and turned around, it twisted Jeffrey's neck with such force that it almost totally severed his brain stem.

The friend in the back seat suffered a torn spleen and lacerations, and the friend from A&M didn't get a scratch. He only had his hearing aids knocked out, but they were not damaged. Everyone was wearing a seat belt and the accident happened only a few blocks from the university.

Jerry called the University Medical Center in Lubbock and was told Jeffrey was in a coma with a severe head injury. They were running tests to see if there was any brain activity. The first report we received was that there was a 10 - 15% chance of survival. While Jerry was on the phone with the hospital, I was busy gathering phone numbers to book flights to Lubbock.

Jerry and I decided we would pack enough clothes for two weeks because I knew Jeffrey would wake up and be alright after that. After all, that's how it is on TV shows. Surely there was some mistake, and things weren't as bad as they were telling us! The doctor kept calling with questions and updates.

I began phoning family and friends asking for prayers. I called two couple friends who lived close by, the EggeBrechts and Burchetts. They were at our house within 15 minutes and remained by our side throughout the rest of the whirlwind night. I called my sister, Dodie, whose husband Lynn was working the night shift in the emergency room in Longview. As a doctor, Lynn could call and gather information that he might understand better than us. I also phoned my friend Deanna in Dallas and left a message. She told me later that she woke up, saw the blinking machine light and decided she should get up and answer it. She was on her knees immediately praying for us.

It was amazing the calmness Jerry, Jamey and I had as we made plans to fly to Lubbock. The time seemed to pass quickly. The earliest flight we could get was out of Hobby Airport at 6:30 a.m., which meant we had to leave before five. As we were getting ready to leave, our friends started asking if we had enough cash to last for whatever length of time we would be gone. Jerry had cashed a $200 check that day, and we had our checkbook and a credit card so we thought we would be fine. They decided to give us more cash. It seemed that Nancy and Betty both had also cashed a $200 check that day. They each gave us money, and combined with what Jerry and I had, we thought we were set for whatever we would face.

It was about 4:15, and I knew I had one more thing to do before we left: go next door and tell Lori. I knew she was home alone, with her husband and son both out of town, but I couldn't leave without telling her. I called, woke her up and told her Jeff had been in an accident and to open her door because I was coming over. We held each other and sobbed. She later told me that after I left, she walked the streets in our subdivision for hours crying. She was trying to comprehend the devastating news and figure out how she was going to tell Brian.

I found out later that Brian had planned to go see Jeffrey that weekend too, but at the last minute had been invited to go to Centenary College in Shreveport, LA, to check out their soccer program. Praise the Lord! Lori said the worst thing she's ever had to do was tell Brian about Jeff's accident. We shared so many memories with those two. She and I joke about getting credit for Jeff's and Brian's baseball ability because we spent hours playing catch with them when they were young.

As we were getting ready to leave, we remembered that Jeff's friend from A&M was involved in this accident too. Jerry called the hospital to gather more information and although we were told the friend was ok, we knew he would need the support of his parents. Jerry called them with the news, so they could make plans to go take care of their son while we took care of ours.

Just as we were leaving, the neurologist called asking permission to drill a hole in Jeff's skull to relieve pressure that was building up on his brain. He told us there was very little brain activity, and now the chance of survival was only 5–10%, so we needed to get there as quickly as possible.

Our friend, Nancy, drove us across town to catch our flight. We rode in silence with the chorus of "Glorify Thy Name" still consuming my mind. I remember trying to figure out the words to the song because it was just the chorus that was playing over and over in my head. I broke the silence in the car as I asked Nancy what the verses said. Startled, she thought for a second and gave me some words. I found out later they were the words to another chorus we sang at church, but they fit so well I was satisfied with her answer.

We arrived at the airport around 6 a.m., and while Jerry bought our tickets, I called our pastor, Damon Shook. He had already received the news and had called the deacon prayer chain to start praying for us. We were already covered in prayer before we even started on this devastating journey.

Once we were on the flight, we all tried desperately to hold it together, only occasionally giving way to a gush of tears. I will never forget Jamey sitting between Jerry and I, softly crying, when a stewardess came by, handed him tissues and went on her way, never saying a word. It was as if people knew there was a crisis going on in our lives, but no one said anything. Everyone was so kind from the very beginning.

Chapter 3

Our Fight to Save Our Son

A family friend picked us up at the airport and we arrived at the hospital at 9:50 a.m. We were met by four members of the hospital staff, including the chaplain. The waiting room outside intensive care was filled with Jeff's friends, along with his friend from A&M, unhurt but visibly shaken. The staff tried to whisk us into the family waiting room to let the chaplain talk to us, but we had to see our son first.

We immediately burst into the ICU unit, and there he was in room #7, with several doctors and nurses tending to him. He was hooked up to a respirator, had a bandage on the right side of his head, and was raised to an almost sitting position. We were looking at him through a glass window in the adjacent room, not realizing there was a patient in there. The doctors looked up, realized who we were, rushed us out of that room, and told us they would come speak with us.

When we had our first conference with the doctor, he told us again there was little hope of survival and not a chance of Jeff being anything but a vegetable. Devastation! We were told that they allowed only two people in an ICU room at a time. Jerry told them there were three of us, so they made an exception. As we were entering the ICU unit, Jamey looked down the hall and said, "Here come the Burchetts." When they had returned home, they decided they needed to be with us and caught a direct flight out of Houston Intercontinental, arriving shortly after we did. What a welcome sight! We will always be grateful they came.

Jerry's relatives, who lived in the area, arrived at the hospital all throughout the day. My sister, Janie, and her husband, Martin, drove up from San Antonio, arriving about three p.m., and my sister, Dodie, and her husband, Lynn, flew in at four o'clock. Along with Jeff and Jamey's friends from Tech, the waiting room was always packed.

We were busy all day with meetings to update us on Jeff's condition. When we weren't talking with doctors, we were standing at his bedside holding his hands, feet, anything we could touch. Jeff's right eye was swollen shut and black and blue. His left eye was open slightly with his eye dilated. His arms stretched down by his sides and his feet extended out. He never moved or responded. We talked to him and loved on him, knowing deep in our hearts that our Jeff was gone, and our lives would forever be changed with a void that nothing could ever fill. But we still weren't ready to give up.

The doctor taking care of Jeff was Dr. Ayeni, head of Neurology at University Medical Center. He was so kind and tried desperately to give us encouragement, yet at the same time be open and honest with us. The nurses in ICU, Carol and Linda, were also incredibly compassionate. It was as if the Lord hand-picked the people He wanted to care for Jeff. They cried with us as they continuously took care of him. A male nurse worked fourteen hours straight, not even taking time to stop and eat. We will always be grateful for the compassion they showed us in letting us all stand around Jeff's bed as they worked around us, only asking us to step out a couple of times while they cared for him and ran tests.

We had only been at the hospital a little over an hour when Jeff's blood pressure dropped, affecting his heartbeat. It was around eleven o'clock a.m. when the doctor called us in for our second of many meetings we would have throughout the day. He told us they were doing everything possible for Jeff, but his body was beginning to shut down, and he could pass away at any time. We were told Jeff's brain was continuing to swell, and the pressure was building.

Jeff's friend from A&M sat motionless, as in shock, most of the time. His dad arrived to be with him. We were so glad because we were really worried about this young man. We tried to assure him we knew it was an accident and did not hold him responsible.

We returned to Jeff's room where the nurses asked us to go get a bite to eat and give them a chance to exchange the respirator mouthpiece for a smaller one. As we sat in the family waiting room, Jerry's cousin's daughter went and bought sandwiches for us. We ate as much as we could force down. We continued throughout the day with meetings and standing around Jeff's bed loving him, talking, and praying, our hearts breaking with fear of what we knew would be the outcome.

The phones were ringing off the wall from coaches, friends, and relatives seeking updates and wanting to fly out to be with us. The strangest thing was the ICU unit turned over their phones for us to use also. Remember, this was in 1990, before cellular phones. The staff told us later that they knew Jeffrey was very special by the feeling they got while taking care of him and the amount of phone calls and people who came to comfort and support us.

One phone call we received was from a friend of Jeff's who was in the Marines and stationed in Virginia. That's how quickly the news had spread. Jeffrey's high school athletic trainer was at the airport ready to come as were the youth director from our church and Jeff's girlfriend and her dad. We didn't know whether to tell them to come or not since Jeffrey was on life support and non-responsive. The doctors were telling us he could pass away at any time. We knew there were only two flights from Houston to Lubbock, one in the morning and one in the afternoon. Being a practical personality, I didn't want anyone to fly out that afternoon and us be gone. It was a very uncertain day filled with unending meetings with different specialists, brain activity tests being run on Jeffrey, updating family and friends back home with information we didn't even understand ourselves, and facing very difficult decisions. Looking back, since we were still in ICU early Sunday morning, we would have said come so they could have said their goodbyes and had closure, but that's the hindsight that's always clearer. Sorry!

After the nurses got Jeff settled again, we let his friends from Tech, who had kept a vigil all night, go in to see him. They were such neat, caring kids, and my heart ached for them. I just wanted to hug them all and make their hurt go away. As Jeff's roommate, James, and I were standing at his bedside with our arms around each other talking, he told me that Jeff was very proud of his family and that he loved us all very much. He told me that Jeff talked about me all the time and had told him he'd never asked me to do anything for him that I hadn't done. That brought a smile to my sad face. While this wasn't totally true, it warmed my heart that he thought it was. Jeffrey did have a way of talking me into just about anything he wanted though.

It brought back memories of Jeff's senior year at Westfield when he would leave class to call me, requesting I deliver Shipley's donuts for him and his friends. He always assured me he had the teacher's permission. On one occasion, I had just shampooed my hair and told him I couldn't go out like that. He pleaded with me and said he would meet me in front of the school. Sure enough, when I pulled up, there he and Randy were, thrilled to get the delivery. I often said if I had to describe my sons with one word each they would be: *Jamey=charming; Jeffrey=charm-er!*

James told me that Jeffrey had shared his adventures with him about all the places he had been and the things he had gotten to do. I remember he was very impressed that one of Jeff's trips was to the Holy Land. I do recall Jeff taking our Holy Land scrapbook back to Tech with him after one of his trips home. As I was remembering that moment with James, I started thinking about all the things that Jeffrey had gotten to do in his nineteen years of life.

He played several sports, which were his number one love. For several years, he and Jamey went to Prude Ranch in West Texas with their friends and cousins. This was a working ranch camp where they were assigned their own horses for the two-week session. They also had a lot of fun on hunting trips with Jerry, their friends, and their friends' dads. We went to Snowmass and Aspen, Colorado snow skiing the week after Christmas for many years with family and friends. He'd been to Disneyland, Disney World, Washington, D.C., deep-sea fishing in Florida, and of course, the Holy Land with a side trip to Austria.

I can honestly say he enjoyed every adventure he went on. James also told me that he and Jeffrey had several conversations about religion, and Jeff had told him he wasn't afraid to die because he knew he would go to Heaven. This too was comforting. The maturity this nineteen-year-old was showing at such a devastating time was amazing, and everything he said was just what I needed to hear.

We continued to have conferences with the doctor where the news was always bleak. We always asked if there was anything else that could be done. The doctor finally told us there was only one more test he could run, sending dye into Jeff's veins. If it went past the brain stem, there was still hope, but if not, death was imminent. We asked him to run the test and call in another doctor for a second opinion so we would know we had tried everything possible to save Jeff's life.

There was always someone around Jeff's bed, whether it was family, relatives, or Jeff's friends. Late on Saturday afternoon, my two sisters, Martha Jane (Janie) and Dodie, nurse Carol, and I were standing on both sides of Jeff's bed, all deep in thought. As I stood there looking at Jeffrey, I silently prayed, "Lord, I don't want him back if he will always be a vegetable." Jeffrey didn't have the personality for that. He was always so active and full of life.

With the nurse working on his IV and me holding his hand, my sister Janie broke the silence and said, "Linda, I know this isn't a good time to bring this up, but have you ever thought about organ donation?" (It seemed she and Dodie had discussed this while I was out of the room.) I said, "No, but good idea."

This was very out of character for me, and it was as if someone else was saying it. There was a peace as I said it though, and I knew it was right. Jeffrey had always been so healthy, and although I didn't realize it at the time, this was the Lord's plan all along, not only for Jeff, but for the recipients as well. I will never forget the look on the nurse's face as she said, "That's great. Not everyone feels that way. The doctor will discuss this with you in your next meeting."

The little conference room was packed with family and friends as the doctor gave us the results of the dye test we had requested. The professor of the Neurology Department at the Medical Center attended also. They both agreed there was nothing else to be done. The doctor seemed to be stumbling around for what to say next when I spoke up and said, "What I think you are trying to do is bring up is the subject of organ donation."

Shocked, he said, "Well, yes, that is something we need to discuss." Jerry was stunned and taken totally by surprise. He immediately started crying and said, "No! I want to take Jeffrey home just like he is." Jamey and I comforted Jerry through tears of our own and then Jamey broke the deafening silence in the room as he spoke up and said, "Why not, Dad? Jeff would have wanted to help others." After about five seconds, Jerry softly said, "Okay, that's what we will do."

It was important for all three of us to agree, or we never would have given permission to be a donor family. We did have questions as to the procedures connected with organ procurement. The doctor explained they handled it with the utmost respect, and it was conducted like a normal surgery. Somehow, through our numbed state of minds, we were satisfied with the answers he was giving us, and we all said okay.

I had discussed the moral side of organ donation and transplants with our pastor, Damon, exactly a year earlier when Jerry's dad was very ill, and we were faced with decisions regarding life support. However, I never dreamed I would someday be making this decision for my child. I was comfortable with the explanation Damon had given me from the moral standpoint, assuring me it would never interfere with God's plan for a life. This played a very important role in the decision we were making now.

Jeffrey had come home from school one day shortly after my discussion with our pastor and asked me what I thought about organ donation. I was able to tell him what he had shared with me. He then told me he and Karen had talked about it, and he was signing his driver's license to be an organ donor. I have no idea what brought about that conversation and didn't question him, never dreaming that a year later he would be one.

I had not thought about this conversation until we got home from Lubbock and Karen reminded me that Jeff had wanted to be an organ donor. This brought a peace and assurance that we did the right thing, and I appreciated her sharing this with me. All I could think of later was, *Wow! The Lord was busy a year earlier putting the pieces in place to accomplish His plan.*

The doctor quickly called in the transplant team, and they came in asking and answering questions. They asked if we wanted to donate Jeff's heart and lungs, and we replied with "anything you can use." They were extremely surprised at our calmness and generosity.

I can assure you that this was the Lord working through us, giving us strength to make these decisions because this was His way of completing His plan for Jeff's life on earth. The Lord knew that we would draw strength and peace through the knowledge that in our devastation and sorrow, we were giving joy and health to many seriously ill people and extra time for Him to complete His plans for their lives.

We signed papers to discontinue life support at 8:20 p.m. on Saturday, March 10, 1990. This began a journey we would have never survived on our own and one where we experienced the presence of the Lord in a way none of us will ever forget. We will be forever grateful and will always give God the glory for not leaving us in the bottom of the pit nor letting us drown in our sorrow, but slowly lifting us up, keeping our heads above water and healing our broken hearts.

Chapter 4

LifeGift Takes Over

The news spread quickly about our decision to disconnect life support. We told the hospital staff that we would stay in the waiting room because we wanted the kids to be able to come in and say their last goodbyes. It was amazing the stillness, sadness, disbelief, yet calmness and strength we all had as we finally came to grips with the inevitable.

The LifeGift staff took over as soon as everyone had said their goodbyes. They quickly worked to keep Jeff's organs functioning while they found suitable recipients. They asked pages of questions about his health and ran a four-hour test, making sure every part of him was healthy. They told us they would try to find compatible recipients in Texas, and everything should be over by six o'clock Sunday morning.

By now it was getting late, and everyone was tired and mentally drained. We decided Janie and Martin, the Burchetts and Lynn would go to the motel and get some rest while Dodie, Jerry, and I would stand vigil at Jeff's bedside. Due to severe bloodshot and burning eyes, we convinced Jerry to go rest a little in the family waiting room. He didn't want to leave so we decided I would go with him, which I did for about thirty minutes. Dodie never left Jeff's bedside.

Jamey went to Jeff's dorm room and counseled about thirty-five kids, letting them talk through their shock and sorrow throughout the night. This was a good venting session for the friends and for Jamey as well. He also let them take anything they wanted of Jeff's. This made it easier to clean his dorm room as there wasn't much left. A day after Jeff's funeral, we received a letter from a girl that was there that night, thanking Jamey for being with them. She wrote that talking about Jeffrey and hearing stories Jamey told comforted them all.

Back at the hospital, it was a long, quiet, somber night. Jeffreys' organs were gradually shutting down, so it was a race against the clock to get the procurement teams in place and on their way. It was another stormy night in Lubbock, and we were under tornado alerts again. This made air flight more difficult and delayed arrivals. There was always someone in Jeff's room, holding his hand and checking his vitals.

At one point in the middle of the night, as Dodie and I were returning from the restroom, we noticed a girl sitting in a squatting position in a chair in the corner of the waiting room. She was the only one in there and she had her hands cupped to her mouth. I thought she was blowing on a piece of tin foil, but Dodie thought she was just blowing into her fists. Whatever she was doing, the sweetest sound of "Amazing Grace" was coming from that corner. We have no idea who she was except a ministering angel that the Lord was continuing to use to help us make it through this drastic situation.

Another example of the Lord's tender mercies was the instrumental music that played over the intercom all night long. We would not be aware of it until a certain song would start to play and then it would be like the volume was cranked up, and the music to "Life Goes On" would fill ICU room #7. It always flooded our minds with a peace that the Lord was present with us.

Sometime during the night, Jeff's nurse was in checking him and I was holding his hand, thinking about how he would never throw a football again or give those good hugs. No longer would he burst through the backdoor yelling, *"Mom, I'm home,"* or *"Mom, you won't believe what happened!"* The LifeGift procurement nurse got two pieces of paper and a pen, and we traced his handprints. She also clipped a piece of his hair for me.

Jeffrey loved clothes and could either look like a GQ ad or a battered homeless person in ragged jeans and shirt. At one point in the night, I told Dodie I would love to know what he had worn the night of the wreck but was afraid to look in the bag they had brought to us because I feared there would be blood on his clothing. (He had a cracked cheekbone that had caused a nosebleed and black eye. There was also a small seatbelt burn on his chest which was the extent of his injuries other than the severe head injury.)

We finally decided that we would look at what he had been wearing. As I carefully took out the clothing they had literally cut off him, I began to smile. To my horror and his delight, he had worn one of his favorite outfits - faded jeans with *holes in the knees,* his long white starched Polo shirt with his white Sperry tennis shoes. Much to my surprise and relief, there was no sign of blood anywhere.

The LifeGift coordinator had worked tirelessly throughout the night to get the perfect recipients in place. Early Sunday morning, everyone was back at the hospital, and it was time to say our last goodbyes to Jeffrey before they took him into surgery. At approximately 8:15 Sunday morning, they asked us to step outside ICU room # 7 as about twelve doctors and nurses surrounded his bed.

As we stood in a line, holding onto and supporting each other, once again the Lord manifested Himself in a way none of us will ever forget. Suddenly, Jeff's ICU room was illuminated with the brightest light we had ever seen, and loud music filled the room. Betty says it was a chorus of angels, and she's probably right because I think this is when the Lord welcomed Jeffrey home to Heaven. The doctors and nurses froze motionless for just a few seconds, then everything went back to normal. We stood softly weeping as they reverently wheeled Jeff past us, through the double doors and into surgery. Next the sobs and hugs came as we knew this was the end of our fight for survival and that our lives would be forever changed.

Janie and Martin left to drive back to San Antonio, and the Burchetts left for the airport. Dodie, Lynn, Jerry, and I decided we would go to the hotel and try to get some rest before our late afternoon flight home. We were told later, Jerry's cousin's husband and their daughter respectfully stayed at the hospital all day Sunday while Jeff was still there in surgery. We appreciated this more than words can say.

Chapter 5

Returning Home From Lubbock

On our flight home, Jamey sat across the aisle from Jerry and me. It was an exceptionally stressful trip, with all three of us trying to keep our emotions intact. I kept looking over to make sure Jamey was okay. Tears were continuously streaming down his cheeks. He was sitting next to a lady that kept looking at him, trying to decide if she should ask him what was wrong. I took a little piece of notepaper, which I still have, and passed it to her. On it I wrote, *"We just lost our nineteen-year-old son in an automobile accident here Fri. p.m. Our twenty-two-year-old son is sitting next to you. Sorry, we have our ups and downs, but we'll be ok. Linda Atkins."* On the back of my note she replied that she was *so sorry. She did not mean to stare, but knew he was upset, and thought he might be alone, and she could help. She wrote that she was a mother and grandmother and again was so sorry about our son."*

We arrived home Sunday evening to a house full of family and friends. When we walked in, you could have heard a pin drop. The kindness and compassion were almost too much to bear. I remember very little of that night except talking to our pastor, Damon Shook, who was there with his wife Jackie. We decided Wednesday would be a good day for the funeral. In hindsight, this was way too soon, especially for the Texas Tech kids that came and missed school and finals. I can only say, when a person is in that kind of unexpected tragedy, it's a miracle they can even think at all. Over the years, when we would say, I wish we would have done this or that differently, we would then have to remind ourselves we did the best we could under the circumstances.

I need to include a special story that really touched our hearts. Friday afternoon, the day before we got news of Jeff's accident and left for Lubbock, Jerry had trimmed all the shrubs in the courtyard thinking he would pick them up the next morning, never dreaming we wouldn't be home. A Ponderosa Forest friend, Tommy Hill, knowing we would have lots of visitors when we returned, brought his lawn mower over to make sure our yard was presentable. He discovered the mess in the courtyard, picked it all up and had everything spotless when we returned. We were so grateful and will never forget his thoughtfulness.

As I was remembering this sweet act of kindness, it brought back a memory of years ago when the boys were in elementary and middle school. Jerry would decide the courtyard shrubs needed trimming, so he would do a superb clipping job, not missing one stray twig. Then it would be the boys' and my job to pick up and bag the trimmings. Inevitably, we would be cleaning it up when Brian from next door would appear and the next thing we'd know, he and Jeffrey would be in the front yard throwing a football or off riding bikes, leaving Jamey and I to do the work. On one such occasion, Jamey and I were working away when he stopped and said, "You know, Mom, Dad is like a tornado. He blows through and leaves all this destruction and then he's gone. We are like the Red Cross. We come through and clean it up!" We so appreciated Tommy for being our "Red Cross."

On Monday morning, we hit the floor running. It was a day filled with appointments, arrangements, and countless decisions we needed to make. The doctors in Lubbock had partially shaved one side of Jeff's head where they drained the fluid from the swelling, so we needed to decide whether to dress him casually with a baseball cap or in the suit he had personally bought when he came home for Karen's Homecoming dance. This would mean buying a wig for him which is what we did. I hated the wig because it didn't fit properly, and Jeffrey had pretty hair which always had to be perfectly styled before he went to school, church or anywhere else. This was another thing I had to get over because the first time we saw him was at the funeral home three hours before visitation on Tuesday night; there was no time to go to plan B.

Word of Jeff's death spread quickly through our church, neighborhood and Westfield High School. People started arriving with food, calling to see what we needed and how they could help. Early Monday morning, a handsome young man who was younger than Jeffrey but played on the varsity football team with him, came over before school to tell us he was big and strong, and if we needed him to carry the casket, he would consider it an honor. This would be another tough decision we would face, choosing friends to be pallbearers. I was so touched by this young man's heartfelt compassion and bravery since we didn't know him well. I will always remember his kindness and willingness to help.

We have a dear friend, Shirley, who owned a small flower shop at the edge of our subdivision where most of the Westfield students got their flowers for prom and other dances. Unbeknownst to us, our pastor had announced in church Sunday morning the news of Jeff's death and to call Shirley for flower orders, saying all proceeds, after expenses, would go into a fund they were setting up for us. She was overwhelmed with orders. As Shirley told us later, her shop was too small to handle all the orders, so the wholesale flower dealer in the Gerland shopping center turned his warehouse over to her. Several school friends and parents from Westfield and Ponderosa, along with Shirley's friends, came to help her and her two employees. She said three or four cars were used to deliver the flowers to the funeral home, and as soon as they returned they filled them up and sent them back. They worked late into the night, needing the assistance of floodlights to see.

Klein Funeral Home told her they had never seen so many flowers, nor had we. We received such unusual and beautiful flowers and plants, such as an arrangement in the shape of a football jersey made of red carnations with the number 9 made of white carnations. Another unusual gift was a beautiful dogwood tree. A friend brought me the Precious Moments figurine of a girl holding a broken heart with a little boy beside her and the inscription, "He's the healer of broken hearts." Another friend gave me a little New Testament with an olive wood cover from a trip she took to the Holy Land. We were given so many sweet and thoughtful gifts that we treasured.

We received word that Channel 11 TV station was sending a reporter out to interview us Tuesday about being a donor family. They also went to Westfield High School and interviewed Coach Emory Bellard, trying to get a glimpse of Jeffrey's personality and character. He had such nice things to say about Jeff and his leadership ability. I will never forget him referring to Jeff as *#9, one of a kind,* and he was!

The reporter who came to our home to interview us was Janet Shamlian, who is now a national correspondent for NBC News. If you are questioning how we could have been sane enough for an interview, we questioned the same thing. It was another example of the Lord lifting us above our circumstances to carry out His purpose and plan. The TV interview provided the organ recipients' families and friends who were at the Houston Medical Center enough information to figure out who their donor was and eventually contact us.

Chapter 6

Funeral Plans

Tuesday was another day of family and friends arriving and our finalizing funeral plans. We had chosen Klein Funeral Home to handle the arrangements and visitation and Earthman Cemetery off I-45 for burial since it was closest to our home. The thing I remember most about that day at Earthman was sitting in a little room with the funeral salesman spreading out a large map of burial spaces.

We were shown several available sections and suddenly I was overcome with grief. I had to get out of there. It was too much to think I was sitting there to choose a place to bury my son. Dodie was with us, so she and I hurriedly left. Jamey and Jerry stayed in the room looking over the map and discussing different options. Jamey chose one he thought had the perfect setting. It had five plots, which we didn't need, but he was so sure it was the right place, Jerry accepted his choice.

We met with our minister of music Tuesday morning to select songs for the service. The first one I knew I wanted sung was the chorus that had consumed and sustained me from the first news of Jeff's accident, "Glorify Thy Name." The audience would sing it along with the hymns, "Amazing Grace," "Because He Lives," and "It Is Well with my Soul."

The last song we chose was one our church choir sang a few months earlier called "Press On." The first time Jerry and I heard it we were so touched by the lyrics that after the service I asked for a copy of the music, never dreaming that I would later request to hear it again at my child's funeral! Our minister of music sang it at the end of the service, and once again we were comforted by the message that when the valley is deep and the mountain is steep, in Jesus' name, we "press on."

After lunch on Tuesday, our friend, Chet Burchett, who had stepped up to act as our liaison to make sure we had met with everyone said the funeral home asked what we wanted in the funeral program. Also, did we want to include anything about organ donation? They needed this information right away. My sister, Dodie, was standing beside me, and I said, "Sure. Dodie write something." As Chet handed her a pen and paper, she gasped and sat down on our stairway. There, she penned the most beautiful description of the gift of life I had ever heard. She sat and thought for a moment, and then the words just flew onto the paper. Incredible!

I also told Chet we wanted Jeff's signature somewhere on the program. The story behind this request was the years he practiced the perfect signature for when he would become a famous athlete. He would fill a sheet of paper with his name all over it. We had his signature on everything in our house. Sometimes he wrote friends' and family members' names too, but mostly just his. He and I had many discussions about what he would become and why his signature would be so important. So, I thought it was only fitting for others to see his signature, but certainly not for the reason any of us would have ever imagined.

The funeral home also wanted to know how many programs we thought would be needed for the funeral. Five hundred sounded like such a high amount. We never dreamed we would need over twice that number.

Jeffrey S. Atkins

To have an abundant life takes some people scores of years to achieve – it took Jeff only 19.

He played his roles in life to the best of his ability and for vast audiences.

He was a child of God, a son, a brother, a grandson, a nephew, a cousin, a team member, a leader.

There was more love and energy and everything good in him than his body could contain, so he shared what he had with all he met and what was received from Jeff is known as a blessing.

In death as in life, Jeff cared, loved, and shared. Donated organs of Jeff's included:

Eyes for viewing God's magnificent creations – the blue skies, green earth, snow covered mountains and clear little streams; the red and black of Westfield's Mustangs and Tech's Red Raiders.

Lungs to breathe in the refreshing air of another wonderful day.

The **heart** to beat in tune with God's plan for a life.

The **liver** to purify.

The **bones** to support.

The **skin** to protect.

Jeff's personal guidelines for an abundant life was also his favorite scripture.

Trust in the Lord with all of your heart and do not lean on your own understanding.

In all your ways acknowledge Him and He will make your paths straight. Proverbs 3:5-6

Jeffrey was a gift, on loan from God, and he will be missed.

We scheduled visitation from six until nine p.m. on Tuesday, March 13. We arrived at 5:30 with people already trickling in. A special surprise was seeing one of Jeffrey's high school Sunday school teachers and his wife. They had moved a couple of years earlier and were at Houston Intercontinental Airport about to catch a flight when the wife saw Jeff's obituary in the newspaper. They immediately changed their flight and came to the visitation.

We were in the receiving line until ten o'clock that night with the last guest leaving a little before 10:30. The number of students, relatives, friends and acquaintances was almost unbelievable. Never in our wildest imaginations would we have expected such a crowd. One thing I remember so vividly was people coming through the line and saying, "I don't know how you are able to stand here and greet people." All I could think to say was, "God's grace is sufficient." We could have never endured such grief without Him carrying us through it.

As we stood in line receiving condolences, I remember thinking, this must be what Heaven will be like. Everyone is so focused, so loving and sincere." I knew there were people there who really didn't like each other, but suddenly it didn't matter. I am convinced there were ministering angels among us too because you could honestly feel the Lord's presence, and we were truly experiencing the peace that passes understanding that the Bible speaks of.

We scheduled the funeral for ten o'clock, Wednesday, March 14. Once again, Channel 11 was there with a TV crew for the evening news. The front of our church was filled with beautiful flowers, and the sanctuary was completely packed. We heard several estimates from 1200-1500 in attendance. The amount really didn't matter, but whatever the correct number was, it was shocking.

We had selected eight of Jeff's friends as pallbearers. The football team and others appointed themselves as honorary pallbearers, something we should have thought of but didn't. Shirley had made a beautiful casket spray of red carnations, and she had the boys take one to wear, which was important to them and to us. Our youth minister, John Wills, read Scripture, and our pastor, Damon Shook, conducted the service. We didn't open it up to spontaneous stories from friends because we were too brokenhearted, needing comfort rather than humor at that time.

The funny stories started coming soon though, like the ones when Jeffrey and his friends would sneak one of our cars out, or climb the radio towers, or jump off our two-story roof into the swimming pool. Parents would be just as well not knowing these, but it was important for his friends to share.

Hearing these stories did clear up one mystery that had remained unsolved for a few years. Jamey had gone to the Houston Rodeo and bought himself a new lariat rope that he kept in the back of his Bronco vehicle. One day he came home to find the rope lying in pieces in the garage. Right away, he accused Jeffrey of ruining his new rope, which Jeff, fearing for his life, quickly denied. Jerry and I certainly didn't know what had happened and Jeffrey wouldn't confess, so Jamey finally gave up but always knew Jeff was guilty.

Jeff's friend, Randy, finally told us about one Saturday afternoon when he and Jeff were at our house alone and bored. Jamey's Bronco was sitting in our driveway just tempting them. Randy convinced Jeff to take it to visit friends in Westador, the subdivision down FM 1960 next to ours. Jeff, being fourteen with no driver's license, finally agreed, knowing he would be in big trouble if he got caught. Off they went to visit their friends, and everything was fine until they started to return home. The Bronco wouldn't start! Oh no! What to do?

There was the answer – the rope! They tied the new rope onto the Bronco and attached it to the bumper of the pickup belonging to a friend of theirs. He would pull them home and all would be well. As they started down busy FM 1960, the rope broke. They stopped, retied it, started up again, and once more, it snapped. It seems that this happened several times before they got the Bronco back home and onto our driveway. Randy's story explained the mystery of how Jamey's new rope ended up in several pieces. Cold case finally solved!

The funeral procession was extremely long and took quite a while to arrive at the cemetery. There we visited with friends we hadn't seen in a long time and receive their love and condolences. It was such a moving sight to see all those young boys file by and toss their carnations on top of Jeff's coffin. Years later, when people talked about the funeral, they would comment that the most touching sight was the number of young people there and how they dealt with losing a good friend at such a young age. It was unlike anything I've ever seen.

We came home from the cemetery to a wonderful lunch provided and served by women in our Sunday school class. Our dear friend, Nancy, worked in our church library and had about fifty tapes of the funeral made and available after the service. They were immediately taken, so she went and made fifty more. It was our hope and prayer that as the kids listened again to the service, they would be convicted of their need for a personal relationship with Jesus. There will be a time in each one's life where they too will face devastating situations and will need the peace and comfort that only Christ can give.

After everyone left, Jerry and I went back to the cemetery for a little while. When we returned, Nancy and Tom were the only ones at our home. Nancy had straightened up our house from the earlier crowd, and Tom was vacuuming our carpet. That was such a touching and sweet visual remembrance we will never forget!

A day or so after Jeff's funeral, our church secretary called to tell us Jeff's heart recipient's family had a pastor friend contact our church to see if there was anything they could do for us. They had seen our interview on TV and had already discovered a lot about us through contacts they had in Houston. The LifeGift people were doing a great job of keeping us informed on the progress of the recipients but weren't allowed to give us any other information. In turn, we kept in touch with the heart recipient's health progress through their pastor friend. We were praying and rooting for the recipients to accept their new organs and have a long life through the second chance they had been given.

Jamey picking out Jeff's grave site

Chapter 7

Back to Reality

Immediately, we opened our home to the kids because they were having a hard time understanding and accepting the reality of losing a friend. We listened, consoled and answered questions as best we could. Jerry and I were so touched by their attention and compassion. In fact, we benefited from these visits as much as the kids did. We thought it especially important to love on Jeff's friend from A&M, assuring him we didn't have any bitter feelings toward him. We could only imagine the guilt he must have experienced. Jerry and I needed him to understand that we believed then, as we do now, that the Lord has a plan for each of our lives, and we can't always understand why things happen as they do, but we can trust and accept.

As we were loving on other people's children, we tried to be especially sensitive to our son, Jamey. We desperately wanted him to know how special he was to us, just as Jeffrey had been. There were so many raw emotions we were all dealing with, and it still seemed like a bad dream.

The week after Jeff's funeral, we received an extremely nice letter from a friend who was an instructor at North Harris County College telling us Jeffrey had been her daughter's first crush when they were in middle school and how well he was liked by other students. In her letter, she told us about a student in her writing class that had written "A Tribute to Jeff" paper that she thought we would benefit from reading. She also stated that because of the student's previous entries, he did not owe her this assignment and he wrote this extra entry out of his love for Jeff. She thought it was a good example to really tell us how our son positively affected the lives of every person who ever knew him. She went on to say that she had told her students she would not share their papers with anyone, so she had called to ask his permission to send us a copy. Thank you for sharing this heartfelt tribute.

Shortly after Jeff's funeral, a neighbor friend came to visit and wanted a copy of all the music from the service, which I happily gave her. A couple months later when her mother was dying of cancer, in such pain and heavily sedated, she discovered the only thing that seemed to calm her was the music from Jeff's service. The last line in the song "Press On" is "with the prize, clear before our eyes, we find the strength to press on." My friend asked me what "the prize" was, and I got to tell her it is eternal life!

We received condolence letters from Texas Tech University, some of Jeff's teachers and his dorm resident assistant. Jeffrey's friends, the residents of the eighth floor of Coleman Hall, purchased several books on humor and architecture they thought Jeff would like for the Texas Tech Library.

In one of the Tech letters, we were told that the flags would be flown at half-staff the first day the students were back from Spring Break in memory of Jeffrey. Also, a short background script of where he was from and what he was studying would be displayed in front of the flags in the information podium. We received calls and pictures from his friends wanting to make sure we knew about it. Very special!

One Sunday night about three weeks after Jeffrey's death, I must have let my guard down just enough for Satan to creep in with doubts of Jeff's salvation. I remember it was like a dark cloud coming over me. I burst into tears and asked Jerry if he was sure Jeffrey was a Christian and if we would see him again in Heaven. Jerry replied, "What are you talking about? Of course, he was!" I responded, "But what if he only had the head knowledge and not the heart knowledge?" Jerry could not believe what was coming out of my mouth, nor could I. He comforted and assured me as best he could and once again, I cried out to the Lord for assurance.

Two days later, we received a letter from a friend of Jeffrey's, who lived in the same dorm at Tech. In his letter he wrote that one thing he admired most about Jeff was the fact that he was a saved

Christian and not ashamed to admit it. They would have discussions about their beliefs with other guys in their dorm. One day not too long before the accident, Jeff told him, and whoever else was in the room, that he was not afraid to die because he knew who his Lord and Savior was and that he had accepted Him into his heart. I was so grateful for this letter and a little ashamed of myself for doubting what I already knew was true.

Family and friends came over each day to help me sort through countless pages of names that needed thank you notes for flowers, food, donations, and gifts. It was truly overwhelming, and I was so appreciative to have their help. I think it took me almost three months to get this all taken care of. As I was writing this book, I became curious as to approximately how many thank you notes were written. We had numbered and alphabetized all the names and what each had done for us, so I quickly tallied them up. On the list I kept, there were three hundred and twenty-eight notes to be written. What a tremendous outpour of love that we will never forget.

Jerry was busy with insurance and other issues, such as going back to Lubbock to get Jeffrey's golf clubs and other personal things that were in his car. He insisted he could go alone, which was one of those huge mistakes we made along the way. It was way too soon, and the wound was too raw. He needed support and our dear friend, Tom, was willing to go with him, but Jerry said no, he thought he would be ok. It proved to be almost too much for him. There was nothing he could do but to take a deep breath and take care of the business he went to do.

One of the issues he took care of was appearing before a judge in Lubbock to get the A&M friend's record cleared. In the state of Texas, if a passenger dies in an automobile accident due to reckless or negligent conduct, the driver is charged with vehicular manslaughter. We did not want this on his record because we knew it was nothing more than a tragic accident. It was quite a process, but Jerry managed to get it done.

Another thing I needed to do but was dreading was to close out Jeff's bank account. I had become friends with one of the ladies at the bank because it seemed like I was always there putting extra money in one of the boys' accounts when they would "accidentally" be overdrawn. I walked in that day and she came over with a big smile and asked which one it was this time? Fighting back my emotions, I told her why I was there. She and I immediately burst into tears, and we embraced right in the middle of the bank lobby. We then went into a side office where we talked and shared memories. Another hard task checked off.

There were so many other things that needed to be finalized. We kept receiving calls to purchase markers for Jeff's grave. We chose black marble as a reminder of the red and black colors of the Westfield Mustangs and Tech's Red Raiders. We would always keep red flowers in each of the end vases.

Next, the decision came as to what inscription to put on the markers. Jamey, Jerry, and I sat down and started discussing different ideas. We decided on a verse from one of the songs we sang at the funeral, "It is Well with my Soul." The verse states, "Whatever my lot, Thou hast taught me to say, it is well, it is well, with my soul." This is exactly how we felt. It wasn't well with our broken hearts, but it was well with our souls because we knew Jeffrey was in Heaven with the Lord and we would see him again someday. This would go on the headstone. We also needed to put something on the footstone. I suggested "Precious memories, how they linger." Jamey began throwing out descriptive adjectives, and this is what we ended up with:

"PRECIOUS MEMORIES......Quick smile, boundless energy, fierce competitor, loyal friend, obedient son, faithful brother, love of life, child of God, silent witness......

HOW THEY LINGER."

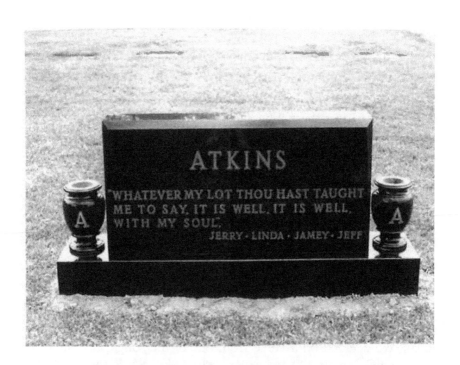

Jerry and I visited Jeff's grave daily. There was an unexplainable peace there, and we could almost feel Jeff's presence with us. There were always notes, souvenirs, poems, pictures, plaques, and things left there by his friends. One such expression of grief was a poem titled, "Silent Rage" written by Jeff's long-time friend, Stephen B. It was such a deep, personal poem you could honestly feel the heartache as you read it.

I decided to place something there for his friends to leave their notes in as they expressed their sadness and worked through their grief. I buried a large coffee can covered with contact paper about halfway down in the ground and kids continuously wrote their feelings down on anything they could find and left them in this can. Jerry and I were always surprised with the response. We left it there for the first year until it was overflowing. They also brought special gifts that meant something to them and to Jeff. Among these items was a little football trophy, a ceramic bunny, some seashells, and a cross that are still there today.

The economy had taken a downward spiral in the mid 80's. In 1989, Jeff's senior year in high school, Jerry made the decision to dissolve our roofing supply businesses, selling one to pay our suppliers and closing the other. With some of our customers being in desperate situations, Jerry had extended credit to them, trying to help save their companies. When they couldn't pay us, that finally led to a situation where we couldn't pay our suppliers. Jerry worked tirelessly trying to secure jobs for our employees with our competitors and other companies.

This was such a sad and unsettling time for our family. Our businesses had been extremely profitable for us, and our employees were like family. We had no idea what the next phase of our life would be but felt certain the Lord would provide and lead us to our next endeavor. After getting the boys settled into Texas Tech in the fall of 1989, Jerry worked diligently into 1990 closing out business accounts. We just thought we knew what loss was until we lost our son that March.

Jerry worked through his grief by making Jeff's grave a beautifully landscaped area. Since he was no longer working and had the time, he poured his heart into his "new" job. He refused to let the cemetery yardmen mow and trim it, never missing a day of going out and checking on things. This bothered a friend of ours, but not me. Our friend thought Jerry was spending way too much time at the cemetery. What he didn't understand was it gave Jerry something to do, and he still felt like he was taking care of our son in some odd way. Also, I always knew where he was. The funeral home director told us later that when they showed people plots to buy, they viewed ours because it was always green and beautiful.

This reminded me of a situation we had with the photograph on Jeff's footstone. We chose the graduation picture of him wearing his red Westfield robe. It started to fade and progressively got worse, so we contacted the manufacturer to tell them of the problem. They had never had this issue, so they asked us to send them the picture again, and they replaced it. After about the third replacement, they asked a very important question. *"Had Jerry been using fertilizer on Jeff's grave and around the footstone?"* Well, yes! They determined when Jerry watered the grass after he'd fertilized, it would get into the porous marble. Sure enough, Jerry stopped fertilizing around the footstone, and it never had to be replaced again!

He continues to care for Jeff's grave, but had to give up the mowing after about ten years because he got too busy with work. He still goes by almost every Friday to check on things, water, and trim when needed.

I remember the first time we went out of town after Jeff died. We needed to go visit my parents in Jefferson, Texas, so they could see for themselves we were alright. We tried desperately to hide how miserable we were. We felt like we shouldn't be there, like something was missing that we had left behind. Thankfully, we were only there for the weekend. I will never forget Mother, Daddy, Jerry, and I standing in a circle in their family room holding hands and Daddy praying for us before we left. As soon as he finished praying, he burst into tears and left the room. After our four-hour trip back to Houston, we went straight to the cemetery before we went home. I still can't explain why, but it was just something we needed to do. Go check on our son!

Family and friends were so kind and attentive, making sure all our needs were met. I don't think I went to the grocery store for a month after Jeffrey died. If someone even thought I was out of anything, they were ringing our doorbell to drop it by. Cards and phone calls continued to minister to us. Some people we knew, some we didn't. We received a beautiful card and note from one of the paramedics with the Medical Center ICU staff. He had stayed over his shift to help take care of Jeffrey. In his note he stated that it is so difficult to understand why tragic events like this happen, but the best we can do is to put our trust in the Lord for all understanding. A portion of Proverbs 3:5, which was Jeffrey's favorite scripture.

A package came in the mail one day, shortly after Jeff's funeral. It was a VCR tape, newspaper clipping, and letter from a baseball coach in League City, whom we had never met. He had been a liver recipient in 1985 and was telling us how grateful he was to his donor for the gift of life and thanking us for being a donor family. The title of his tape was "Twice Blessed." In his letter, he told us that ten days after his transplant he attended his daughter's graduation, later had seen his son make All-State Baseball two years in a row and was currently preparing to leave on a five-week fishing trip. He had never met his donor family but was so grateful and thanking them through us.

Another letter we received was in the form of a thank you from a gentleman in our subdivision. His daughter was a classmate of Jeff's, and he had received a heart transplant two years earlier at Methodist Hospital in Houston. He too was grateful to have seen his daughter graduate and later celebrate his 25th wedding anniversary. He had not met his donor either, and this was his way of thanking them through us. I totally understand their gratitude.

My sister, Dodie, was working in Longview as an oncology nurse at the time of Jeff's death. She would work all week and leave at six a.m. on Saturday mornings to be in our driveway by ten. She did this for six weeks straight. Her presence each week was such a comfort to us. If she was five minutes late, Jerry would pace the floor, wondering where she was. She assured us that it brought as much healing to her as it did to us. She was such a blessing. As a side note, my sister, Janie, came and stayed a week with me, helping get my thank you notes organized. She and our brother, Steve, both had children at home ranging in ages from two years old to high school. They were equally as loving and supportive to us, as were our parents and Jerry's family as well.

Dodie and Jeffrey had a special bond. She often said watching him grow up was like watching me all over again. He would stand beside me in front of a mirror and ask why people thought we looked alike. I would reply that if he put a wig on, he would look just like my school pictures. He was never impressed.

As I mentioned before, Dodie was an excellent oncology nurse. She treated her patients like they were family and loved them through their journeys with cancer, rejoicing with cures and weeping with losses. Since she had captive audiences while her patients received their hours of treatment, she shared about her nephew's life, how he became an organ donor, and how the Lord was helping us all deal with our grief. She was such a powerful witness during this time.

About six weeks after Jeff's death, I had the overpowering desire to get the clothes he had worn the night of the accident and sew them back together. Remember the night in the hospital when I had wanted to check out Jeff's clothes but was afraid there would be blood on them, and when I finally looked, there wasn't? As I was piecing together his shirt, I noticed an orange-yellow color around the collar and down the front of his otherwise spotless white shirt. I thought it must be some medicine they had used on him that I had not noticed the night I inspected it in the hospital. I pieced everything together and put the clothes away.

Six weeks later, (three months after Jeff's death) I once again got out his clothes just to hold. This time, I noticed the spotless white shirt that had changed to orange stains after six weeks had now turned to dried blood. I couldn't believe my eyes. I called Dodie, who had witnessed the totally white shirt the night in the hospital and told her of my discovery. She too was speechless. It suddenly was very apparent that the Lord doesn't give you more than you can handle, and he had blinded our eyes to the blood that I'm sure was there all the time. Thank you, Lord, for this small favor!

We kept in contact with Jeff's friends at Tech, assuring them we were okay and making sure they were as well. We received many notes, letters, and calls from them, wanting us to come visit. So, Wednesday, April 25, six-and-a-half weeks after Jeff's accident, we drove to Lubbock.

We checked into our hotel room and since it was late, decided to wait until the next day to contact Jeff's friends.

We got up early and drove over to Plainview, Jerry's hometown, to visit with his relatives. On the way back to Lubbock, Jerry agreed to take me to the wrecker yard so I could see Jeff's car. It was sitting on the end of a row, and we got out and looked it over one more time. Parked across from it was one of the cars they had hit that night. The hood was up on that car and for some reason I went over and looked at it. Stuck to the motor was the missing T from the Texas Tech sign Jeffrey had on the back windshield of his car. I peeled it off and brought it home with me.

We returned to Lubbock after lunch and called Jeff's roommate James. He wanted us to come over to the dorm. We were apprehensive about going to Jeff's room again but decided we could do it. We did fine and for some reason, it was good to be there. We visited with James and other friends in their dorm. The kids were excited and so were we, although it was bittersweet for all of us. Jerry and I had planned on taking the kids out to dinner and told them to invite whomever they wanted. We decided James would contact the boys, and I would call the girls. They would pick a restaurant and we would all meet there at eight p.m. As we were leaving to go back to our hotel, our car broke down, so we went to a repair shop where we ended up leaving it overnight for a new fan belt and water pump. We were so thankful it didn't break while we were driving to Lubbock the previous evening.

At dinner, we met a room full of the neatest college kids you could ever find. They had gotten us a separate room at a restaurant and the tables were set up in a square so everyone could see each other. We talked, letting each friend tell where they had met Jeff and anything else they would like to share. I explained to them that the only way we were able to survive was because of our relationship with the Lord. I told them the importance of a close bond with their families and how crucial a personal relationship with the Lord was because you never knew what you would face each new day. Once again, the Lord enabled us to enjoy ourselves in a very difficult situation.

We asked the kids if there was something of Jeffrey's they would like to have. A couple of them wanted T-shirts, which we sent back to them when we returned home. One friend requested one of Jeff's Calvin and Hobbs shirts because he thought Calvin had a very mischievous look like he was up to something. It reminded him of Jeff because he was always up to something too. Another friend wanted a T-shirt which was practically torn up but still had a neck on it to hold it together. It was so ridiculous, but Jeffrey loved to wear it. We had a very enjoyable evening and were glad we went. A couple of the Tech kids came to visit over the summer, which we were grateful for and enjoyed very much.

The Missing "T"

41

Chapter 8

Beginning our "Firsts"

As you all know, when you lose a loved one there are all of those "firsts" you must get through. Our first holiday after Jeff's death was Easter. Even as teenagers and young adults, he and Jamey still received Easter Baskets full of candy and gifts. I wouldn't be filling Jeffrey's basket with goodies this year but would be remembering him with flowers. Off I went to Walmart to get Easter Lilies for his grave. As I passed by the Easter display of baskets, candy, and bunnies with all the mothers shopping for their children, a sudden sadness came over me with the realization that I too should be buying those things. Before I knew it, I was overcome with grief, burst into tears, and ran out of the store.

Easter Sunday, Jerry and I went to Sunday school and church as usual. Looking back, I should have stayed home. Sitting in Sunday school, memories flooded my mind and tears started streaming down my face. I finally got up and went to the restroom to try to get control of my emotions. As I stood by the door with my back against the wall, a well-meaning friend came in, saw me and realized what was going on. Trying to comfort me, she told me to not be sad because Jeffrey was with the Lord. This is easier said than done because *"We know where he is, and we know where he is not, he isn't here with us, and we are sad!"* This was a quote from my sister Janie after being told the same thing so many times. I have always thought it was the perfect answer, and it still makes me smile visualizing her saying this. I finally got a grip and made it through church.

Easter Sunday evening, Louie Giglio was preaching at First Baptist Church in Houston. Nancy and Tom drove us down to hear him. Their daughter, Whitney, was a student at Baylor and a friend of Louie and his wife, Shelley. At the time, he was teaching at Choice

Ministry at Baylor with hundreds of students attending each Monday night. Louie knew of our situation through Whitney but had no idea we were in the audience that Easter Sunday night.

His message was about the trials and troubles in a Christian's life. Jerry and I were glued to his every word as if we were the only two there. His message challenged us to continually praise God no matter what. He went on to say that we would all walk into trials, but were we prepared to walk through them? He recounted that when his dad had been gravely ill, the song "Jesus, Name Above All Names" had been like a chorus singing in his mind. Also, he shared that everything his dad had ever made became so precious to him. Oh, how I could relate!

He encouraged that the only way we would be able to walk through a trial was to keep our eyes on the Lord, keeping God between us and our problem. He then gave a hand illustration explaining how we can't handle things if we look at our situation through our own eyes (closed hand in front of our eyes). However, we can handle it if we see it through the Lord's eyes (fingers spread apart). I can't tell you how many times I recalled this illustration and would place my hand in front of my eyes, spreading my fingers apart to see my grief through the Lord's eyes.

We found out later that Nancy and Tom were concerned that our emotions were too raw for such a message. Louie ended his sermon by going from A to Z naming the attributes of God! It was such an encouraging and incredible evening.

Not long after Easter, Jerry and I went to Waco with Nancy and Tom to attend one of Louie's Choice services. We had planned to go one week but had to postpone it to the next. One of the songs Louie had chosen for the night we had originally planned to attend was "Glorify Thy Name." Afterward, we were talking with Louie when I told him how that chorus had ministered to me from the beginning of our journey. Startled, he shared with us that when he was selecting the songs the previous week, "Glorify Thy Name" kept coming to his mind. He said they hadn't sung that song in a long time, but for some reason he decided to include it, not having any clue we might be there. The Lord knew it was too soon for us to sit through that song, so He postponed our trip for a week.

I shared with Louie how his Easter Sunday message had been such a help and encouragement to Jerry and me. Again, he said he had no idea we would be in that service, or he might not have said some of the things he did. This was another example of the Lord knowing exactly what we needed and when we needed it.

The next "first" was Mother's Day. Sweet memories of funny cards and gifts the boys had given me through the years raced through my mind. Jamey used to get so aggravated with Jeffrey because Jeff always felt the need to tell me how much money they had spent on my presents. Jamey was so glad when they got old enough to each buy separate gifts. I received phone calls and gifts from Jeffrey's friends and from family members. I got beautiful flowers and lots of hugs from Jamey that year. Everyone tried so hard to make me feel loved and I was so appreciative of all their thoughtfulness.

We received a phone call from Coach Emory Bellard telling us that the coaches and staff at Westfield High School had decided to remember Jeffrey by renaming the varsity locker room. They placed a plaque over the door that read "The Jeff Atkins Varsity Locker Room. In Memory of a True Mustang Spirit." They called us to come down to the locker room after it was installed to have our pictures taken. One of Jeff's friends went by about five years ago and told us it is still there. We were so grateful for their thoughtfulness.

The LifeGift liaison did an excellent job of keeping us informed about the progress of Jeff's organ recipients. It seemed everyone was doing well except the heart recipient. Remember, his family is the one who had the minister contact us through our church to ask if there was anything they could do for our family. We had been given his name and phone number, so we immediately called him to find out what was going on. It seems the recipient was having other medical problems that were causing stress on his new heart. We kept in constant contact with the minister and on Wednesday, May 23, two and a half months after receiving Jeff's heart, his recipient passed from this life into the loving arms of his Savior, Jesus Christ.

We were heartbroken for his family. We found out his name was Thad Woziwodski from Colorado Springs, Colorado. His funeral would be on Saturday, May 26, at Village Seven Presbyterian Church at one p.m. Jerry and I were torn on what to do. We desperately wanted to attend his funeral but were afraid it was not appropriate to do so. We stewed over this, going back and forth, trying to decide if we should go or not since we had never met this family and did not know what their reaction would be. Our friends, Tom and Nancy, told us if we decided to go, they would go with us - we were not to go alone! One thing we knew for certain we wanted to do was send flowers. We decided on a beautiful heart-shaped arrangement signed from Linda, Jerry, and Jamey Atkins, Thad's donor family.

In our last conversation with the go-between minister, he assured us it would be fine with Thad's family if we attended. He encouraged us to not worry about what other people thought and to just follow our hearts in making this decision. Our hearts said to go, so we called our friends, and they said, "We're ready, but there's only one catch." Their son, Wade, was a senior in high school, and our church was hosting a reception for seniors and their parents at noon on Sunday, so they would need to be back for that. One of the mistakes we made, that I referred to previously in wishing we had done things differently, was to drive to Colorado Springs instead of flying. It sounded like a reasonable idea at the time, with no hassle of finding last minute tickets or getting to the airport and renting a car. The only problem was by the time we decided to go it was noon on Friday, and the funeral was the next day. Off the four of us went, driving straight through until we arrived in Colorado Springs. We checked into a motel to grab a couple hours of sleep before the funeral.

We arrived at the church early, sitting off to the side, with no one realizing who we were. It was a beautiful service and mirrored Jeffrey's with almost the exact same song selections. One of the officiants at Thad's funeral was his friend, pastor and Christian author, Dr. John MacArthur Jr. I own one of his books Our Sufficiency in Christ. I never dreamed I would one day meet him in person, and certainly not at one of his friend's funerals. Another officiant was Thad's home church pastor, Reverend A. Bernhard Kuiper. The pallbearers were three successful business friends from Houston, along with the Woziwodski's three sons.

We decided to go to the graveside service and leave from there to drive back to Houston. This is where we met everyone. I remember us trying to decide if we should walk down the little hill to join the family or stay off to ourselves. It seemed all eyes were on us since we were strangers. We decided to walk down and join the family. When they found out who we were, they were overcome with gratitude that we were there. Thank you, Lord! They were grateful to meet us, and we were so happy to meet all of them, only wishing it had been under different circumstances. They wanted us to go to their home to visit, but we told them we had to be back in Houston by noon Sunday.

When they found out we had driven all night only to turn around and drive back, they were astounded. They told us if they had only known we were coming, they would have sent a company plane to bring us! Oh well. It all worked out, and we had a good time being with our friends. We made it back just in time for the reception and have always been grateful that we followed our hearts and made the right decision to go.

At the end of May, when Jeff's friend, Karen, graduated from Westfield, Jerry and I felt like we should attend the ceremony. It was on Sunday afternoon in Huntsville, which is an hour's drive from Houston. Karen's family had asked us to go out to dinner with them that evening. After graduation, we arrived back home at five, with an hour to spare before we met them for dinner at six.

As I sat in the car gathering up the Sunday newspaper along with my purse, Jerry walked down our driveway to the edge of our yard to turn on the sprinkler system. As he leaned over, two young men appeared, stuck a gun to his head and demanded his wallet and jewelry. Jerry told them to calm down and that he would cooperate. He gave them his wallet, gold Rolex watch, Texas Tech class ring, and an initial ring. They took no money because it was in his money clip that he kept in his front pocket.

Knowing I was still in the car and that I would get out at any minute, Jerry attempted to distract the robbers by walking across the front yard toward the street. The unarmed young man yelled to the one with the gun, "Shoot him, shoot him." Thankfully, the one with the gun didn't shoot and told Jerry to get back on the driveway, which he did. Sure enough, about this time, having no idea what had just taken place, I opened my car door and stepped out with my arms full of stuff. Jerry yelled for me to get back in the car, and like any wife would do, I asked, "Why?" That was when I noticed the two men and vividly saw the shiny silver gun pointed at Jerry. Shocked, I turned to get back in the car when Jerry changed his mind and yelled, "No, get in the house," as he started up the driveway towards me. (He told me later that all he could think of was keeping himself between me and the gunman long enough for me to get to safety.) Startled when they saw me, the two thieves didn't know what to do so they took off running. We have no idea if someone was waiting for them in a car or where they went.

Of course, we called the police, went downtown the next day to give a description, and later back to observe a lineup, but they were never caught nor were any of Jerry's things recovered. Once again, news spread quickly up and down our street regarding our harrowing situation. We were all so shocked and couldn't believe Jerry was robbed in broad daylight in our own front yard.

We calmed down and met Karen and her parents as planned. About nine p.m. our doorbell rang. It was a young mother who lived down the street holding a warm loaf of banana nut bread. She hugged me and said she didn't know what else to do so she made us a treat. So sweet and so very thoughtful!

Chapter 9

Working Through Grief

Everyone works their way through the grieving process differently. Lori recalls the many times her doorbell rang, and I would be standing there with tears in my eyes. We would go sit by the curb to talk and cry. I also remember the many times I went two doors down to the Smiths who were so kind and compassionate as they listened to me pour out my heart in disbelief. They lived on the other side of Lori and had watched our kids grow up. They also had lost a twenty-one-year old son on Christmas Eve years earlier and could identify with what we were going through.

Jamey was dealing with Jeff's death the best he could, keeping busy with work and trying to make sense of losing his brother as reality set in. Friends from church kept calling to invite him to go to First Baptist Houston Monday night Bible study with them, but he kept refusing to go. I was beginning to grow concerned about him, and although I understood anger and disbelief are stages of grief, I certainly didn't want him to dwell there. I almost insisted he try it. Finally, he gave in and went.

After a few weeks, he was asked to speak about Jeff and organ donation to the Bible study group. I read a copy of a letter he had written regarding that night recently. In the letter he said he had arrived early, and the musicians were deciding on the music for the night. He said they needed one more song, so he asked if they would sing "Glorify Thy Name." They agreed that it would fit perfectly with the other songs. He remembered they were sitting in a circle, and his song was the last to be sung. They were all singing, being led by Jamey's friend, Shelley, and accompanied by a guitarist. About halfway through the song, everyone except Shelley, including the guitarist, had stopped singing. He said it was like the Holy Spirit filled her, and he had never heard anything remotely like it. Tears flowed; healing had begun. Thank you, Lord!

These friends invited him to go to a Baylor football game with them that fall. He came back and asked me if I knew the Cannons that went to our church. I told him I did as they were in our Sunday school class. He started telling me about meeting their daughter, Rachel. Little did we know that seven years later, she would become our daughter-in-law. Amazing how the Lord works!

We received so many cards with such sweet notes and messages that I just couldn't throw any of them away. I decided to open the cards and put them in clear plastic pages in binders so I could reread them when I needed encouragement. After months of doing just this and putting as many as I could on a page, I ended up with three binders full of beautiful cards and notes. Some of the cards were from people we did not know personally but who had heard of our loss from others. We also received cards from people who had been given the gift of life through other donors.

My dad was in the hospital for a knee operation while I was completing my card project, and I was staying in his room helping care for him. While he slept, I worked on my card books. As the nurses came in to check on him, they asked what I was doing. It gave me a wonderful tool to share with them the death of our precious son and how the Lord had swept us up in His loving arms and was carrying us through this heartbreaking loss.

We also received numerous books on grief. It was a few months before I could concentrate enough to read any of them. Some were helpful, some not so much. One book that had a great message for all of us was "Are You Weeping with Me, God?" It was written by a mother who had lost her nineteen-year-old daughter in an accident. She was stuck in the angry stage and was terribly mad at God. Her turning point was the day she received a well-intended copy of a religious magazine from a friend. As she turned the pages of the magazine, she read about one miracle after another, where at the last minute, God had stepped in and saved someone from certain death or tragedy. She felt herself lose control, burst into tears and throw the magazine as far as she could across the room. She dropped to her knees, and cried out to God saying, she too could have written a story telling readers of God's glory, if she had received a miracle!

She said that within an instant, it was like a movie camera focused on a slow-moving parade. She started seeing her daughter's life play through her mind, showing her many times that the Lord had saved her daughter, such as the time she almost drowned. This was the starting point where she began to thank the Lord for the nineteen years she had her daughter, rather than the time cut short without her.

As I read this passage, it reminded me of the time Jeffrey was about one and a half years old, and we were living in Alief, next door to Sonny and Nancy Wilson. It was early afternoon, storming outside, and we were under tornado alerts. Jeffrey started choking, and I couldn't get him to catch his breath and keep it. Frantic, I ran next door with him and Jamey. Nancy loaded us and her two kids into her car and drove us to the emergency room in pouring rain. Each time Jeff lost his breath, I would nearly beat him to death trying to get him to catch it. Through the storm, through the night, several x-rays and hours later, it was discovered he had swallowed part of an orange crayon.

Another miracle was when Jeff had an extremely high temperature and started hallucinating in the car on the way to the doctor. I was very frightened and later relieved to arrive at the doctor's office and get the help we needed. These were just two times that quickly came to my mind. After hearing tales from Jeff's friends of daring things they had done, I'm sure there is a long list of times the Lord spared his life. We are forever grateful for the years we had to love and nurture him. Thank You, Lord.

As I remember those early days and months when we were working through our grief, there were many times we would be sitting in church, alone with our thoughts. The words to a beautiful song or meaningful message would trigger tears to well up in my eyes. I would struggle so much not to cry. I tried every trick I could think of, such as holding my breath, rolling my eyes, pinching myself, and even biting my tongue to divert my sadness, but nothing worked.

Once the tears started, Jerry and the whole row of friends would join in. I'm surprised anyone would sit with us because this happened time and time again.

Our friend, Shirley, shared with me recently that shortly after Jeffrey died, Jamey went to her house to talk about Jeff. Jamey shared with her that he felt like our family was living in a fish bowl. I told her he had said the same thing to us, and I had agreed with him. All eyes were on us, watching to see if we were "walking the talk."

I will never forget the first time the three of us went out to eat. It was so heartbreaking to have an empty chair at our table. We walked in and spoke to some friends who were there with another couple we did not know. I noticed our friend lean over and whisper something as they all looked over at us. I knew what had been shared, but I also understood we all want to put a face with a story.

I was asked many times after Jeff's death to give my testimony, and I always said that the Lord has a plan for each of our lives. His ways are not our ways, but He is kind, compassionate, faithful and trustworthy to see us through any situation we face. I believed that on March 10, 1990, and I believe it today! I don't ever want to give the impression that we had it all together at all times, because that is the farthest thing from the truth. There were many days I felt like I was in the bottom of a pit, and I would call out to the Lord to pull me up; He did, little by little. There were days that it would have been so much easier to simply lie down on the sofa and stay there, drowning in my sorrow, but praise the Lord I didn't! I always found it interesting that when Jerry would have a terribly sad and down day, I would be up, and on days I would be down, he would be up.

All of us, at one time or another, have said or done things we deeply regret and would love to undo. Jerry and I were trying to return some normalcy into our lives, so we signed up to host a dinner party in our home through our Sunday school class. It was on a Saturday night and there were six couples, including us. One of the couples was new to our class and had no idea we had lost our son a few months earlier. The men were eating in the dining room, and the women were in the kitchen.

To this day, I don't know why the new lady started talking about organ donation, but for about fifteen minutes, I sat in horror listening as she said that no one should ever sign up to be a donor or agree for a family member to be one. The other four ladies at our table sort of got stiff and sat motionless without saying a word. The lady sitting next to me kept patting me on the knee underneath the table. I didn't want to embarrass the new lady, so I also said nothing, thinking she would end her rant any minute, but she didn't. I went to the dining room to see if the men needed anything and when I returned she was still going strong, saying that once you sign papers to be a donor, the doctors give up on you. You are no longer a priority because all they think about is getting your organs. Her husband was an attorney, and she assured everyone she knew what she was talking about. I guess she never noticed the tears in my eyes, but everyone else did as I desperately tried to control my emotions. Finally, she finished, we had dessert, and they all left.

As soon as they were all out the door, I began sobbing hysterically and asking, "Did we do the right thing? Did we give up on Jeffrey?" Poor Jerry, having no idea what had taken place at the kitchen table, started trying to figure out what in the world was wrong with me. I finally calmed down enough to tell him the story. Once again, he reminded me of everything I already knew to be true, and we cleaned up the dishes and went to bed.

The next morning when we got to Sunday school, the new lady was standing at the door of our classroom waiting for me. With tears in *her* eyes, she told me how terribly sorry she was for all the things she had said the night before, and that she had no idea we had lost a son and were a donor family. I told her I totally understood how we all say things in innocence that are hurtful to others and that I forgave her. We hugged and later became good friends. It seems that when they all left the night before, the four ladies who were so familiar with our situation had waited for her and bombarded her with the facts of our journey. I will never know what was said in our front yard that night, but it was a good lesson for all of us.

Once again, the Lord sent me a reassuring message on Monday afternoon when I received a phone call from the LifeGift procurement nurse in Lubbock. She called to check on us, and I shared with her what had happened on Saturday night. She carefully and compassionately went over all the details and I was again convinced we had made the right decision.

Along with getting back to "normal," Lori and I once again went back to volunteering at the hospital. We were fine unless our shift included dismissing a new mother and her baby. If the baby was a boy, we were sunk. We couldn't look at one another because we would fight back tears until we settled them into their car. This took a while to get over.

I remember being at the hospital one Monday morning when our day chairman was talking to a lady who was there to visit one of her ill friends. She called me over to ask if I had ever met the visiting lady. I replied no, but then suddenly realized this was the lady who went to our church who had lost her son two years earlier when he and friends were returning from a spring break mission trip. They were hit head-on, and her son was killed. I remembered it well because, along with our church family, I had grieved for them, not knowing them personally. I recalled trying to reconcile how God would allow these young people doing His work to have a fatal accident. We stood there talking and sharing, and I will never forget thinking, *It's been two years since her son died, and she still cries at the mention of his name.*

I had this same thought while talking to a lady who was our church receptionist at the time. Years earlier, while she and her husband were serving as missionaries, her son was tragically killed. It had been eighteen years since her son died, and she still cried when she spoke about him. In the conversation with her, she gave me good advice that I will never forget. She said, "Your broken heart has to heal from the inside out. You can't just put a bandage on it and think everything will be okay, because it will just fester and become worse. You should continually put healing salve in it, the Lord's Word and

His promises, and it will heal properly." She told me that there would always be a scar, but the wound would slowly mend.

I also observed that when my mother-in-law talked about her precious son, Bobby Gene, she always cried. This was her first-born child, who was four years older than Jerry. He had been born with a terrible birth defect, rendering him totally helpless. He had lived to be ten years old due to the loving care he received. Mom grieved the death of her child until the day she died at age ninety-four. I know now the Lord gave me these examples because He knew that I too would cry on occasion when memories of Jeff caught me totally off guard and flooded my mind.

This recently happened to me was when I was standing in line at Walmart, thinking of the Harvey flood victims and how our simple acts of kindness were so appreciated. Suddenly, I was reminded of the notes from parents we had received after Jeff's death telling us of the times he would be driving through our neighborhood and see young kids playing football at the park or in their front yards and would stop to play with them. The parents were so impressed and appreciative of his thoughtfulness to their children. I felt tears well up in my eyes and I thought, *Oh no! This can't be happening!* Sure enough, tears started streaming down my face as I quickly paid for my groceries and left. I thought, *Twenty-eight years later, and I still cry.*

My sister, Dodie, told me that soon after Jeff's death she was struggling to understand why the Lord had let Jeff die since the week before his accident I had asked Him to please not let me lose either of my boys because I was sure I wouldn't survive. A week later, Jeff was gone. My only answer is in the Bible we read that the Lord's ways are not our ways, nor His thoughts our thoughts. I also know He never makes mistakes. The Lord will use any means He wants to bring about His perfect plans, not only for our lives, but for the lives of others. I would not have survived on my own strength, but I did only by the Lord loving and carrying me until I was ready to walk on my own again. The Bible also promises that He will not leave us comfortless, and He will always meet our needs. I know this to be true.

I've often been asked questions regarding the healing process and if it ever does get better. Yes, time really is great healing medicine. I have thought about this a lot, and I decided years ago that it takes two years before you are not consumed with the loss of your loved one, wondering how it could possibly be true. I think it takes about five years before you accept the situation and focus not on the loss, but the wonderful memories you have tucked away in your heart that no one can ever take from you.

It was now July, and we had kept busy with family get-togethers and birthday celebrations. At the end of the month, Jerry and I decided we would return to Plainview for his high school reunion. Since Plainview is only an hour's drive from Lubbock, he agreed that while he and his friends were attending the daytime activities, I would drive to Lubbock to visit the hospital nurses and LifeGift liaison I had become friends with during Jeff's stay at the Medical Center. I would return later and meet him for the dinner dance that evening. This would give me another chance to tell the nurses and staff how grateful we were for the care and attention they had given our family and friends during that dreadful time when Jeffrey was there.

What Jerry didn't know, but I had planned to do, was go view Jeff's car again to see if it would bring closure of some sort. I really don't know what benefit I thought it would bring, but I was determined to see it again anyway. A family friend was in summer school at Tech and agreed to go with me. I picked her up and away we went to the junkyard Jerry and I had gone to in April. I went to the space where the car was parked before, but it was not there. I drove up and down the rows of wrecked cars but couldn't find it.

The attendant came out of his office to ask if we needed help. I told him we were looking for my son's car and described it to him. He told me that the car had been sold the month before and was not there. I had never in my life experienced rage, but I did that day. I can't explain what came over me, except I think if I had been there alone, I would have torn into that attendant with all the might I could have mustered. I'm sure I would have been arrested for assault. The anger

I was experiencing was so unlike me. It was as if the last bit of Jeffrey had been taken away from me forever. I screamed at him, *"What do you mean you sold it? It was my son's car, and it was wrecked and no good!"* He sarcastically replied, *"The engine was still good ma'am, and besides, it wasn't your car anymore. The insurance paid you for it!"* Shocked, heartbroken and defeated, I got back into our car, took our friend back to her apartment and went back to Plainview.

Chapter 10

A New School Year

It was time for school to start again, and Jeff's friends were stopping by to visit one last time before returning to their various campuses. Memories of the year before when Jeffrey was so excited to leave for college, meet new friends, and start a new chapter in his life, flooded my mind. Once again, I cried out to the Lord to give me peace and strength to deal with these memories and to replace the sadness with the happiness Jeff had experienced the short time he was at Tech. The Lord faithfully answered my prayers.

Jerry and I had kept our Westfield Mustang season tickets as did other parents we had spent so many Friday nights with when our boys were playing football together. Chet Burchett was the game announcer, and at the first game of the 1990-91 season, he paid tribute to Jeffrey. Friends of ours had gotten together to pay for a beautiful, full page ad in the program in memory of Jeff. Chet asked the audience to please stand, turn to page five in their programs, and read the tribute while he gave personal insight into Jeffrey's character. Jerry and I stood holding onto each other to get us through this tribute without collapsing into hysterical sadness as memories flooded our minds.

JEFF ATKINS

Join with me in a moment of tribute to the memory of Jeffrey Scott Atkins, WHS Class of '89. Jeff was a freshman at Texas Tech last March when he was so suddenly taken from his family and friends by an unfortunate automobile accident.

Traditionally, such an occasion would be observed by a moment of silence. I would rather recall for a moment some of those attributes Jeff had which make him so delightfully memorable to all who had the pleasure of knowing him and watching him grow up with such a zest for life.

Jeff was the starting QB for the Mustangs in 1987 and 1988. He was a leader on and off the field because of his personality, strength of character, and fierce desire to excel in every aspect of his life's endeavors.

Two years ago tonight, Jeff led his teammates onto the field to begin competition in District 15-5A football. He believed his team could win and helped instill that belief in his teammates -WHS finishing district play with 5 wins, 1 loss (to District Champions Huntsville) and one tie – being co-runners-up with Humble.

It was young men like Jeff who established a winning tradition at WHS. It is their memory which guide today's athletes.

Jeff didn't mind that the opponent might be bigger or faster than he was. He just assumed that kind of helped even the odds for the other team.

Those of us who knew Jeff will always miss him.

Those of you who didn't know Jeff missed a real treat!

(Written and presented by Chet Burchett before the football game Friday, September 28, 1990)

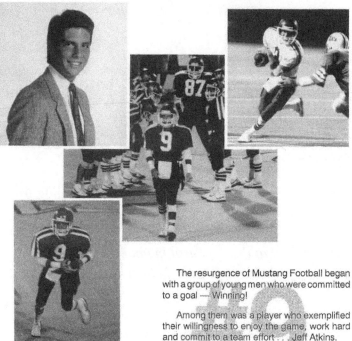

JEFF ATKINS
CLASS OF '89
OCTOBER 26, 1970 — MARCH 10, 1990

The resurgence of Mustang Football began with a group of young men who were committed to a goal — Winning!

Among them was a player who exemplified their willingness to enjoy the game, work hard and commit to a team effort . . . Jeff Atkins.

His efforts at Westfield High School instilled leadership and pride that all admired. He left us all too soon.

MUSTANG VARSITY QUARTERBACK
1986-1989

I was reminded of the many times we sat in those very seats watching Jeffrey and his friends play football. Countless times my brother and sister-in-law brought their three sons, Matt, Greg, and Brian to watch him play. Their boys were nine, seven, and almost two. Jeffrey loved for them to visit so he could show them off, and they adored being with their cousin Jeff. I remember one time we were keeping them, and Matt and Greg were going outside to play football. As they walked out the door, Matt yelled, "I'm Atkins, #9." Greg yelled, "I'm Speaks, #23." Those were such fun times, so long ago. By the way, Matt is now a successful football coach.

It was now September, and I went to visit my friend Deanna in Dallas. Jerry called me one night with the news he had just received a call from Jeff's liver recipient. We were very shocked, but excited. He had given Jerry his name, Karl, and his phone number. Jerry told him I was out of town but would call and visit with him when I returned. I could hardly wait to go back home and make that phone call.

After talking with Karl, it sparked a deep desire to locate the other recipients as well. In July, I had written a letter to the recipients telling them who we were and how we became a donor family. I also shared about their donor, and that we were praying for them to recover and lead a healthy, happy life. I wrote that we would love to hear from them if they wished, sending our names and phone number in the letter. I sent it to the LifeGift liaison, who was our go-between since they were not allowed to give us names or other information except health updates. She eventually forwarded my letter on to all the recipients. This is how Karl got our phone number and called us.

We then received a letter from the kidney recipient's wife telling us about him, their family, and how he was very involved in the National Kidney Foundation in Austin. Although she did not give us their last name, she said his first name was Jimmy. This was enough information for my sister Dodie and I to make a trip to Austin, track him down, and meet him and his family.

A short time later, we received a letter from the lung recipient with only the name Rob signed at the end. He said he lived in North Dallas. It would not be until the next April that I would find out his last name and talk to him.

Trust in the Lord with all your heart, and lean not on your own understandings, in all your ways acknowledge him and he shall direct your paths.

Proverbs 3:56

Jeff Jenkins

Chapter 11

My New Assignment

We continued to receive encouraging cards, phone calls, visits and flowers as we got through Jeff's birthday and Thanksgiving. I had been accepting invitations to share my testimony to ladies' gatherings and Bible study groups. I also received calls from friends who knew someone who had lost a child, and I would call them. I could not believe I had been thrown into this arena. I'm not comfortable talking to people I don't know, and I'm certainly not a public speaker. Even in school, it scared me to death to have to speak in front of a crowd.

Although I'm always terrified, I've never said no, nor will I. I think it's the Lord's way of keeping me on my knees and totally depending on Him to get me through each sharing session. All I can ever do is share with others how the Lord got us through Jeff's death. When asked to call someone who has lost a child, I'm always reminded that everyone's situation is different, and every parent thinks their child was unique and more special than anyone else's. So was mine.

We made it to December, and as I shared before, we were so grateful that the Lord sent us the Christmas tag to let us know He was aware of our broken hearts. That little tag was a reminder that His promise is true that He will not leave us comfortless. After we decorated our home for Christmas that year, I bought a small, artificial tree to take out to the cemetery. I decorated it with sports ornaments, and Jerry secured it at Jeff's footstone the best he could.

I went out a couple of days later, and it was gone. This is the second time I felt rage but certainly not as badly as the first time. I could not believe it and stormed up to the cemetery office crying my eyes out as I told them my son's Christmas tree had been stolen. The people in the office didn't know what to do with me. They were so sorry and said they tried to patrol the premises as best they could, but these things happen. I finally left after I realized there was nothing they were going to do or really could do.

Jerry and I decided we would go to our Sunday school Christmas party, which would be in a small, private room of a restaurant. When we arrived, the room was full of tables for four that were relatively close together. There were several people there and each table we saw already had four people, so we sat at one up front. A couple came in and sat at our table until someone they knew better arrived, and they moved to sit with them. Now Jerry and I sat at a table alone, leaving us with that "fish bowl" feeling.

After we had eaten, it was time for the entertainment. A young lady from our church began to sing Christmas songs. Wouldn't you know, she stood right in front of our table, and her first song was, "I'll be Home for Christmas." I still shake my head in disbelief thinking about that night. It was awful. Of course, tears started streaming down our cheeks as we tried desperately not to collapse into sobs of sorrow. We thought the entertainment would never end so we could get out of there and let our tears freely flow. What a terrible memory.

I'm sure some of you already know how healing it is to write down your feelings, whether it's for your benefit only or for someone else's. Jamey had done this when we were asked to write a letter about Jeffrey to the insurance company, and I had experienced it when I sent a letter to Jeff's recipients.

Soon after Jeff's death, I went up to his room, opened his desk drawers and found folder after folder of letters, journals, papers, and scriptures he had written. They suddenly became so precious as we read in his high school papers of his dreams for the future. He wanted to be a successful architect, buy a ranch, get married, and have three children. In one of his papers, he even told what he wanted to name his children - Kyle, Lauren Ashley, and Keifer! One of the scripture verses he had written in calligraphy was his favorite, Proverbs 3:5-6. *"Trust in the Lord with all your heart, Lean not on your own understanding. In all your ways acknowledge Him, and He will direct your path."* We decided to make copies of this and give it to family and friends for Christmas. I don't know how many we made and framed that year, but it was a lot.

In one of his high school journals he wrote, *"There are two certain people that I would like to model my life after. The first would have to be Jesus Christ. I'm a Christian and I'm not ashamed to tell anyone. There are certain times when things weren't going right that I feel that I couldn't make it through without Him in my life. The second person would have to be my father. He is a big influence in my life and has good morals."*

I remembered all the stories we were told of the times Jeffrey witnessed to people beginning in high school. He told them he was a Christian and wasn't ashamed to say he knew he was going to Heaven. Of our two sons, I had always thought of Jamey being the boldest about his faith, because this was his personality. I had heard before that some kids even called Jamey "The Preacher" because of his witnessing. I did know that when Jeffrey was a sophomore in high school, he came in one night and asked if he could buy his girlfriend a new Bible. I guess I was always so aware of Jeff's busy, active, fun-loving lifestyle, I didn't pay a lot of attention to his serious side.

I had been told once by a coach that Jeffrey was confident and cocky, but those were good characteristics to have in a leader. Some of his new Tech friends repeated this, but they also said it didn't take long to see the real Jeffrey emerge and to become long-lasting friends. We also received notes from kids that wrote they weren't in his group of friends but that he had always been very nice to them and made them feel special. I began to understand that the Lord knew Jeff didn't have much time left, so He had put him in a leadership role and was using him to witness to others. In reading the things Jeff wrote in his journals, we discovered his favorite food (pizza), favorite colors (red and black), favorite activity (football), and favorite song ("Life's Been Good"). It was indeed!

In January, I got a call from a friend asking if I would go down to the Houston Medical Center with her to talk to one of her friends whose son was desperately ill. I found out the young man, who was a classmate of Jeff's, had contracted an infection in the lining of his brain right before Christmas. He was in a coma. I learned that he had been active in the band at Westfield and was a very popular kid with the band students and their parents. Since Jeffrey played sports and our group of friends were parents of kids in athletics, our paths had never crossed, and I had never met the young man or his parents. As I said before, I've never said no, but for some reason, I really dreaded this visit. Our situations were so different. My son had died, but hers had been in a coma for a month now and was still fighting for his life. I had no idea what to expect.

When we arrived, the little waiting room was filled with their friends. Some I knew, most I didn't, but they all were expecting me to share something that would help their friend cope. Not knowing a lot about her son's condition, I made the terrible mistake of asking her if the doctors had given them any hope of recovery, which I thought was a reasonable question since the doctors in Lubbock were always honest with us. That's when she exploded, screaming that there is always hope! She went into a rant that I sort of just blocked out, knowing I had asked the wrong question, and there was no need to try to explain what I meant. I also knew where she was coming from since we tried everything we could before we gave up hope on Jeffrey. Her son died two months later, having never regained consciousness. I reached out to her afterward, and we had several good visits. We kept in touch until she moved away.

Soon would be our first Valentine's Day without Jeff and exactly a year from his last visit home. Such memories flooded my mind. Lori and I decided we would send care packages to our friends' children who were away at college. I sent them to Jeff's friends at Tech also. It was quite an ordeal as we made several types of cookies and mailed twenty-two care packages that year. Our Sunday school class expressed their continued love and support by putting flowers in the church worship center in memory of Jeffrey and the young man who lost his life the weekend before Jeff. It was a sweet and thoughtful surprise.

For I am already
being poured out as
a drink offering, and
the time of my
departure has come.

I have fought the
good fight, I have
finished the course,

I have kept the faith;

in the future there is
laid up for me the
crown of righteousness,
which the Lord, the
righteous Judge, will
award to me on that
day; and not only to
me, but also to all
who have loved

His appearing.

II Timothy 4:6-8

Jeff Jenkins

Chapter 12

Back to Lubbock

It was now March, and we were grateful to have survived our first year. At the same time, we dreaded all the memories we would relive. We received so many calls, flowers, and letters that year it was amazing. The love and support were truly overwhelming.

We were still in contact with Jeff's friends at Texas Tech, and they once again asked us to come visit them. It had been exactly a year since we were there the last April, so we decided to go. We told them to pick a restaurant, invite whomever they wanted to, and we would take them out to dinner again. This time we decided to fly instead of drive, not realizing how difficult it would be. So many memories came back as we arrived in the Lubbock airport for the first time since Jeff's accident. We landed, got off the plane and collapsed into each other's arms. We seriously considered getting back on the plane and returning home. The memories were almost too much to bear.

As usual, we regrouped, rented a car, and went to our hotel. The kids were already calling us, and a couple of them arrived at our hotel room shortly after we did. We went back to the same restaurant with most of the kids that were there last spring. There were a couple of new ones, and we were missing some that didn't return to school or couldn't come for various reasons. Once again, we enjoyed being with them, catching up on their activities, and letting them know we were doing okay.

While we were there, I contacted the LifeGift Liaison, whom I had become friends with, and she had a special surprise for us. It was National Donor Month, and she had used Jeffrey's story, picture, and *signature* as an advertisement with large displays at the two hospitals and the shopping mall. The title of the display was *"Leave More Than Your Footprints."* Along with Jeffrey's donor story, she had a picture and article of a one-year -old boy who was a heart recipient. It was well done and a sweet surprise for us.

As I visited with Sylva, I told her about meeting the heart recipient's family, the liver recipient, and the kidney recipient. I told her we had received a letter from the lung recipient in Dallas, knew his first name was Rob, but did not know his last name. Once again, she reminded me she was not allowed to give out information. Eventually, I found out his last name and then knew the names of four of Jeff's recipients.

While we were in Lubbock, we visited the Medical Center to see Jeffrey's name on their new Tree of Life. My siblings had donated money to purchase a leaf engraved with his name in his memory. Another beautiful and meaningful moment for us.

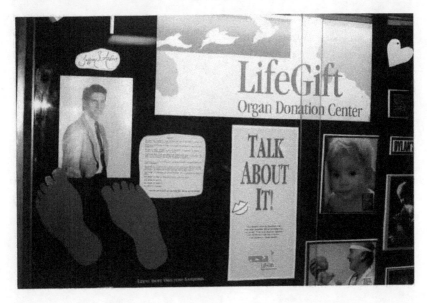

Chapter 13

Life Goes On

Another Easter, another Mother's Day, and friends and family still remembered us with cards, calls, and gifts. July approached, and it was birthday month for Jerry and me, along with our 25th wedding anniversary. As I was reminiscing about past birthday cards I had received from the boys, I remembered a particularly funny one that Jeffrey had given me when he was fifteen. On the front was a cartoon picture of a boy and his mother with the caption, *"Hey Mom, remember all the aggravation I've caused you?"* On the inside it said, *"I'm almost done!"* At the time, we all got a good laugh not ever realizing what a true statement that would be.

My siblings threw us a 25th Anniversary party in San Antonio where my sister Janie and her family lived. This would be another bittersweet celebration because the one that would have had the most fun wouldn't be there, but we were determined to make the most of it. They rented a dinner cruise boat, and we floated down the San Antonio River along the walkway, while eating delicious Mexican food. We later returned to their home for dessert and skits.

We had such a fun weekend and appreciated their effort in celebrating us and helping with the healing process of getting back to enjoying normal things. The song that kept playing over the intercom at the hospital during Jeff's night in ICU, *"Life Goes On"* is so true. Life really does go on and we have a choice to either get on board or live a sad, miserable life. The days and months continued to fly by. The Lord continued to heal our broken hearts by using friends and family to help us through the healing process. We were still amazed at all the loving care we received.

In December, we got a very sweet surprise when we received a Christmas card from the LifeGift Organ Donation Center of West Texas. They had used the tribute highlighting organ donation that my sister, Dodie, had written for Jeff's funeral program as the inside of their card. We felt proud and honored. In tiny print at the bottom of the card it said Jeffrey's sister wrote the tribute for her brother instead of his aunt for her nephew. Sorry, Dodie.

A tremendous blessing happened a couple of years after Jeff's death. This is a wonderful example of how the Lord makes sure you know what He's up to. One Friday afternoon, as I was volunteering at the hospital, another volunteer began talking about friends of hers with the same last name as a young man who played football with Jeff. It being a rather unusual name, I asked if she knew Jeff's friend, and she said yes. I told her the young man was a friend of Jeff's, and although he was younger, they had played football together at Westfield. I didn't think much more about it at the time.

The next evening, we had Coach Bellard, his wife, Mary Kay, and the Burchetts over for dinner. The guys were talking football, and suddenly this young man's name came up again. Coach Bellard began saying what a good player and outstanding young man he was. We all agreed, still not thinking much about it.

The next afternoon, I went to a wedding shower where I started talking to a pretty, young lady that I had not previously known. She told me her last name, which was the same as Jeff's friend. Once again, I asked if she knew the young man. She said that yes, he was her brother, and they were both going to be baptized at our church that night. When returning home from the shower, I told Jerry we needed to be on time to the evening service because Jeff's teammate and sister were going to be baptized. As Pastor Gary Aylor was preparing to baptize Jeff's friend, he asked him when he asked Jesus into his heart. He replied it was at his friend's funeral. It finally became clear why for the last three days, the Lord had made sure this young man's name was on our minds, so we would know others were saved because of Jeff's death.

Another surprise happened on Jeff's twenty-first birthday when Jerry and I took flowers to his grave. Jerry had planted a non-fruit bearing purple leaf plum tree at Jeff's gravesite. These trees produce beautiful flowers that bloom in the spring. Jeff's birthday was October 26 and on the trunk of the tiny tree was one beautiful blossom. I couldn't believe it, nor will I ever forget. What a wonderful birthday present from the Lord.

The Lord continued to surprise us by using others to give us special blessings. In 1993, we received a phone call from our nephew, Lynn Bourdon III, asking if we would care if he and his wife, Susan, named the baby boy they were expecting after our Jeffrey. We were so surprised and felt honored at this request. It's been such a joy to watch him grow into the nice young man he is, and someday soon he'll be a successful attorney.

Another family surprise came a couple of years ago, when another nephew, Matthew DonCarlos and his wife, Amanda, announced they were having their second son also naming him Jeffrey. He is so adorable and is active just like the Jeffrey he was named after. I know our Jeff would be so honored and excited over these namesakes.

We received a notice from the National Kidney Foundation informing us they were making quilts that would be on display around the United States and asking if we would like to submit a block or two in memory of Jeffrey. Jerry's mom had been making all her grandchildren quilts, so we decided she would quilt Jeff a square, and we would send it along with information about Jeff. She made a very pretty one and when it was traveling through our area, we went to see it. It was a sweet and heart-wrenching thing to see all those memories so lovingly made into a quilt.

We have three personal friends who lost young adult children within five years of Jeffrey's death, and another one a few years later. We grieved so deeply with them, knowing the journey they were about to embark on. Three of them are buried in the same cemetery as Jeff. One was Lori's thirty-year-old niece, who used to babysit for us on occasion. She fought a hard battle with cancer and is buried close to Jeffrey.

I was listening to the news one night when I heard about a young policeman who had stopped a man on the Hardy Toll Road. The man exited his car, started running, and the policeman chased him. Suddenly, the man turned around, fatally shooting the policeman. I laid awake that night grieving for the parents of this twenty-five-year-old policeman whom I had never met, but I knew the heartache his family was going to experience.

Much to our surprise, the young policeman was buried right in front of Jeffrey. Jerry and his dad have spent many hours caring for their sons' graves. They became good friends, sharing stories about their sons as they each continued to work through the healing process.

MERRY CHRISTMAS

* Recipients

LifeGift
Organ Donation Center
of West Texas

Jeffrey

To have an abundant life takes some people scores of years to achieve-it took Jeff only 19.

He played his roles in life to the best of his ability and for vast audiences.

He was a child of God, a son, a brother, a grandson, a nephew, a cousin, a team member, and a leader.

There was more love and energy and everything good in him than his body could contain, so he shared what he had with all he met and what was received from Jeff is known as a blessing.

In death, as in life, Jeff cared, loved, and shared. Donated organs of Jeff included:

His *eyes* for viewing God's magnificent creations - the blue skies, green earth, snow covered mountains, clear little streams; the red and black of Westfield's Mustangs and Tech's Red Raiders.

His *lungs* to breathe in the refreshing air of another wonderful day.

His *heart* to beat in tune with God's plan for life.

His *liver* to purify.

His *bones* to support.

His *skin* to protect.

Merry Christmas
From The LifeGift Staff

Jeffrey was a gift, on loan from God, and he will be missed.

(Reprinted with permission from Jeffrey's sister who wrote this tribute to her brother.)

Chapter 14

The Recipients

This is a part of our journey that I've never shared but always wanted to. I tried once, and the Lord taught me a lesson I will never forget.

One Monday night, in August of 1995, I was asked to give my testimony at a ladies Bible study at Gail Brown's home. I decided I would share how we came to be a donor family and what I knew about the recipients. By this time, we had met two of them in person, one's family, and talked to a fourth. Each one had a wonderful story. I piddled around most of the day thinking over exactly what I would share that night.

Late that afternoon, I decided I would go upstairs to gather correspondence and prepare what I would say. As I started to look for the letters and pictures we had received, I couldn't find any. When I sat down to make my outline, my mind was blank. I grabbed my Bible to at least find appropriate scriptures, and it was like I was staring at blank pages. I knew there were highlighted scriptures in my Bible, but I could see none nor think of where to find one. I started looking for outlines from previous talks because I knew I had written scriptures on them. Again, I couldn't find any. I started to panic.

Suddenly, the Lord spoke to me as clear as day saying, *"I'm not sending you over there for you to share what you did for others, but what I did for you!"* Shocked and frantic, I didn't know what to do. Jerry was out of town and I was all alone in a terrible situation. It was now after six o'clock, and I was scheduled to be at Gail's at seven. I ran to the phone to call my friend Betty Burchett. By now, I was crying almost to the extent of hysteria. Betty listened as I told her what had happened. We cried, laughed, prayed, and I cried some more, because I was running out of time. At twenty minutes until seven, she said, "Go powder your nose, get yourself over there, and I will pray." I went. She prayed. I have no idea what I shared that night, but I received a note, four years later, and things suddenly became crystal clear.

In September 1999, a group of young people were having a prayer rally in a church in Fort Worth, Texas, when a crazed gunman entered and began shooting. Seven young people were killed, one being a twenty-three-year-old young lady. I didn't know her, her family or any of the others, but I grieved for the families who lost loved ones in such a senseless act of violence.

A couple of months later, Gail brought me a thank you note she had received from the young lady's mother, Stephanie, thanking Gail for the donations she and her husband had given in memory of her daughter, Kim. In her note she wrote, *"I still remember quite a few years back when I went to a Bible study that you were leading, Gail. That night you also had a gal share about losing her son. Do you remember? I remember it touching my heart-and know now it was another way that God was preparing me for the "advance" of my daughter to Heaven."* I couldn't believe what I was reading. What a valuable lesson I learned from this.

Recently, I was attending a Bible study at church, and this lady was in the same class. She gave *her* testimony, telling of "The Light Still Shines" ministry where she shares her daughter's testimony. After all these years, this was the first time I had ever met her, and I showed her the note she had written that I still carry in my Bible. I identified myself as being the one who shared that night about losing my son. She was so surprised and told me she still remembered my words. I don't recall much about that night, but I certainly remember the hours leading up to it. This time, I think I have the Lord's blessing in sharing the stories of Jeff's recipients with you.

First, I would like to share with you an article written for National Donor month by the LifeGift coordinator, Sylva Zella, who worked throughout the night matching up suitable recipients. This was the beginning of our journey in becoming a donor family.

LEAVE MORE THAN YOUR FOOTPRINTS
Sylva Zella RN/BSN CNRN

It was late, and I was tired when the hospital called. "Can you come talk to this family about organ donation?" Of course. That's my job. "I'll be right there," I said, and immediately got dressed and left for the hospital. I forgot about being tired as I reviewed the facts in my mind. The patient was a 19-year-old freshman at Tech who had been in a head-on collision the night before. He had just been pronounced brain dead by the physician and his family was interested in more information about donating. What do I say to them? Do I tell them that there are 22,000 people on the waiting list for transplants and 33% of these will die before they receive an organ? No. The people needing transplantation are not the problem of this family. Their priority, and rightly so, is their son. I know. It happened to me. I am a donor mom as well as an Organ Donor Coordinator for LifeGift Organ Donation Center of West Texas. Offering the option of organ and tissue donation to the families of potential donors is not only my job but was also experienced by me when I lost my 12-year-old daughter to brain death after an accident. Because of this experience, I feel that I can offer the families a great deal of compassion and personal support as well as the option to donate.

The hospital lights loomed as I pulled into the parking lot. I put all thoughts of my daughter aside and within minutes I was in the intensive care unit reviewing the patient's chart and talking with the nurse who called me. She filled me in on the details of the accident and what had occured since Jeffrey's admission to the surgical intensive care unit. My potential donor now had a name. Jeff. A solid, strong name. Now it was time to meet his parents and talk to them about donation. As I walked into the private waiting room, I took a deep breath. I knew how this felt. Jeffrey's mother, Linda, was holding herself in tight control with tears at the edge of her eyes, while his father, Jerry, was holding his head in his hands, visibly upset. After introductions were made, I told Linda and Jerry that I knew how they

*felt and why. They both gave me hugs and began to tell me about Jeff.
He was a freshman at Texas Tech majoring in Architecture, was a
member of many clubs and had already made lots of good friends.
As I talked with them, he began to take on character and definition,
becoming already much more than just a "patient." They understood
that brain death is irreversible, and Jeff was already gone. They felt
that he would have wanted to give everything he could so that others
could live. They wanted something "good" to come out of such a
terrible tragedy. As they signed the consent form for donation, my
heart went out to these parents who were giving the gift of life to so
many others at a time of their greatest loss. What loving and caring
people!*

*Now began one of the most complex, difficult, and yet, one of the
most rewarding experiences I have ever had. It was up to me to locate
recipients for all of Jeffrey's organs and tissues, while managing his
care in the unit. My first call was to the United Network for Organ
Sharing in Richmond, Virginia, which is the National Scientific
Registry for all patients in the United States needing transplant.
They sent me a list of all the patients who matched Jeff's blood type,
height and weight, with the most critically ill patients printing out
first. After calling Marilyn Haight, RN, the local Lion's Eye Bank
Coordinator, and arranging for eye donation, I began calling to find
recipients, according to the UNOS list. This process took hours, but
I managed to find recipients for his heart, lung, kidneys and liver.
Each recipient transplant center sent a surgeon and team to Lubbock
to recover the organs and take them back to their patients, so we had
four surgical teams on their way.*

*During this procedure of multiple phone calls and patient
management, Linda, Jerry and other family members kept a quiet
vigil at Jeff's bedside. At one point, Linda and I traced the outline
of his hand on a piece of paper for a keepsake. Jeff's aunt, Dodie,
and I cut a lock of his hair and put it in an envelope for the family
to take home. There was always a family member sitting next to the*

bed holding Jeff's hand, usually mom. I knew how she felt. Memories pressed on me as I remembered how hard it was for me to let go of my daughter's hand. Linda and I just held each other and cried and cried.

Time became short. The surgeons had arrived and it was time to move Jeffrey to surgery. The entire family gathered to say goodbye to the young man who had been an inspiration and a beacon in their lives. Tears flowed and hugs were given. I told Linda and Jerry that I would send them a letter letting them know something about the recipients and how they were doing, and then it was time to leave. I gave a final hug to this loving family who had captured not only my heart, but also the hearts of all the staff in the unit.

The first information letter we received from the LifeGift Center was expressing their sympathy and thanking us for thinking of others in our time of great loss. They then shared with us some preliminary information about the recipients.

"Jeffrey's heart was transplanted in Houston, to a 52-year-old architect who had two previous heart surgeries, the last failing in November of 1989. His heart had begun to decompensate and was so critically ill that he had less than 24 hours to live when he received this transplant. He's married, has five children, and is recovering well at this time.

A 39-year-old male investment broker attorney from Dallas received the lung in Houston. He is still in ICU, but no longer is on the ventilator and breathing fine, therefore, his recuperation is progressing nicely. He is married but has no children.

Jeffrey's liver was transplanted in Houston to a critically ill 32-year-old nuclear power plant builder, who is recovering well at this time.

A 29-year-old male computer specialist received the left kidney. He is married with one daughter and runs a mile every day. You might be interested in knowing that he is Chairman of the Texas Kidney Foundation. Now he is out of intensive care and is recuperating normally. The right kidney was sent to Dallas, but unfortunately was unable to be utilized for transplant.

Each of Jeffrey's corneas were transplanted here in Lubbock to a 75-year-old woman and a 90-year-old farmer, who are both doing well. They hope to see their grandchildren soon."

Heart recipient – Thaddeus Miron Woziwodzki
June 8, 1937 – May 23, 1990

The trip to Colorado Springs to Jeff's heart recipient's funeral started a wonderful relationship with his widow, Carmen, by correspondence and telephone calls. She wanted to know all about Jeffrey, and I wanted to know all about Thad. At her request, I sent her pictures of Jeff, copies of papers he had written, and the program of his funeral service, along with a letter telling of Jeff's background and personality.

In turn, she sent me pictures and articles about Thad's background, career path, interests, and personality. She also sent me a letter she had written to their friends, titled "A Miracle," about Jeff being Thad's heart donor, which was further confirmation that we made the right choice to attend Thad's funeral. I would like to share Carmen's letter with you.

"A Miracle"

"The parents of Jeff Atkins, who was the donor, giving his heart to my beloved Thad, March 11, 1990, were at Thad's funeral May 16, 1990. A complete surprise! Through truly miraculous events, we were aware of this precious family since two days after the transplant and were so thankful to God to be able to pray for them. However, the Lord

blessed us in an even greater way. This dear family came to share in our loss and they gave us a tape of Jeff's Service of Remembrance, which was attended by 1500 people in Houston, Texas. Jeff gave his life to the Lord in 1981 and loved the Lord, desiring to model his life after the Savior's. He wrote this in a paper as a senior in high school. When I listened to the tape and the testimonies about Jeff, I wept thanking God for this most precious gift to us.

Thad and Jeff were both committed to Christ. Jeff was studying to be an architect. He was able to be one for two months, giving precious life to his brother in the Lord, Thad, who was a fine architect for 30 years. Five men prayed to receive Christ as their Savior at Thad's bedside. God accomplished so much through my dearest, beloved Thad and this dearly loved son of Jerry and Linda Atkins and brother of Jamey.

Thad's and my deepest prayer was – "Lord, could you send us the tender heart of a believer." He did, and He revealed it to us – Praise be to our Lord and Savior Jesus Christ.

These events have God's fingerprints all over them. Donors and organ recipients are never introduced to one another by name or otherwise. The Lord did it and because He lives, Thad and Jeff live also, and I can't wait to be reunited with them.
In Christ's Name, Carmen"

Through corresponding with Carmen and reading newspaper articles, we learned Thad was born in Gostyn, Poland, emigrated to Jersey City, New Jersey, in 1961, and moved to Colorado Springs, Colorado in 1965. He was a very successful architect, being Chairman of the Board/CEO of the Woziwodzki Group, a Colorado Springs-based architectural firm with branch offices in New York City and Los Angeles. We learned he was the consulting architect overseeing construction on skyscrapers in several major cities, including Denver, Colorado. After my sister, Dodie, heard this, she found and bought me a small gold charm in a shop at the Denver airport that is a replica of the Denver skyline. Every time I wear it, I think of Thad and Jeffrey. Such a treasure.

Carmen sent me a copy of Thad's impressive corporate brochure. I loved reading of his accomplishments and seeing pictures of him doing what he loved. Thad also was a racing buff. In 1981, he drove the Pikes Peak Hill Climb, then a year later, as a sponsor, he combined with Bobby Unser Jr. to win the hill climb championship three times in the next five years. Jeffrey would have been so impressed.

Carmen and I talked on the phone several times during those early years and exchanged correspondence by mail. During one of our phone conversations, she shared with me that due to harsh winters in Colorado, a lot of people put special blankets on their loved one's graves, which she had done on Thad's. When she and her daughter removed it in the spring, the grass was dead everywhere except one place where it was green in the shape of a heart. She said they couldn't believe it, nor could I. She was so grateful that the Lord was continuing to show His love and mercy in healing their broken hearts.

The last time I heard from Carmen was a Christmas card photo she sent us in 1994. She had fallen in love with a wonderful Christian man, and they had married in July. It was a family photo where they all looked extremely happy, and we were thrilled she had found love again.

Thaddeus M. Woziwodzki, A.I.A., ranked among the nation's most experienced and respected architects. He had more than 30 years of accomplishments in the architectural, engineering, construction, and financing fields.

Mr. Woziwodzki graduated from the Technical School of Building Construction in Poznan, Poland, and from Warsaw Polytechnic, Architectural Division in Warsaw. To Escape communist constraints, he emigrated to Jersey City, N.J., in 1961, where he began to study architectural design And construction management at the Vito Batista School of Design in Brooklyn and the Pratt Institute in Philadelphia. He moved to Colorado Springs in 1965 and founded the firm in 1977.

Thad's professional skill and years of hard work combined with the loyalty of clients led to The Woziwodzki Group's becoming a mature international consulting firm with projects spanning from Australia to Yugoslavia, before his untimely death in 1990 from heart disease.

Liver recipient - Karl Cockrell

January 24, 1957 – November 24, 1999

After mailing a letter to Jeffrey's recipients in July 1990 through LifeGift, giving them our names and phone number if they were interested in contacting us, Karl was the first to call. During my first conversation with him, we talked for a long time, and he told me how he came to be added to the transplant list. He had contracted Hepatitis C from eating raw oysters that had destroyed his liver, causing him to become desperately ill. He told me he was born and raised in Bay City, Texas, had three brothers, and had played football in high school. He had been in and out of the hospital several times and was eventually told a liver transplant was his only hope. Since he was too ill to work, he was staying with his mom and dad, waiting for the call to go to Houston for his transplant.

During our conversation, he shared something with me that he hoped would not upset me. He told me that on *Saturday afternoon, March 10,* he was watching TV. Suddenly, this inner voice started repeating *"Pack your bags - tomorrow's the day"* over and over in his head. He finally jumped up and started packing. His mom came into his room and asked what he was doing. He told her about the inner voice telling him to pack his bags because he was getting his transplant the next day, so he was getting ready. Sure enough, *Sunday morning, March 11,* around six a.m., he got the call to go to the Houston Medical Center for his transplant. Wow!

What is so amazing about this story is we didn't sign consent papers until *8:20 p.m. Saturday night,* and the inner voice spoke to Karl *Saturday afternoon.* I've always wondered if this was about the same time on Saturday afternoon that my sister asked me about being a donor family, and I said, "Good idea." I'll never know for sure, but once again I was reminded that the Lord has a plan for each of our lives, and He is already aware of how it's going to work out.

As I was talking to Karl about our family, I shared with him that Dodie was an oncology nurse at Good Shepherd Hospital in

Longview, TX. We discovered that his grandmother, who lived in Carthage, TX, had cancer and was being treated in Longview. On his grandmother's next trip for treatment, Karl went with her and met my sister for the first time. He brought pictures of his family, which Dodie forwarded on to us. We kept in touch by phone on a regular basis.

He wanted to come to Sunday school and church with us, so we said okay. He arrived early that Sunday morning, and although I had been excited to meet him in person, it felt sort of strange to have him in our home. He was such a likeable guy that we quickly adjusted and left for church. The next time we would see him in person was Thanksgiving at my parents' home in Jefferson. He was visiting his grandmother in Carthage, which is about an hour away, and asked if he could come meet the rest of our family. We again said okay. This is the only recipient that Jamey and Jerry met in person. While they liked updates and were praying for them to recover and live happy, healthy lives, it was too sad and too soon to become best friends.

I continued to keep in contact with him and often talked to his mother at length. In one conversation, I learned that one of Karl's brothers had been killed in a train/car accident in Bay City. I grieved with her over the loss of her son. Over the years, Karl would have setbacks trying to keep his medicines leveled out and would be hospitalized from time to time. I remember visiting him a couple of times when he was back in Methodist Hospital in Houston. Finally, nine years and nine months after receiving his new lease on life, he passed away. Dodie and I visited his grave in Bay City to pay our respects and say goodbye.

Kidney Recipient – Jimmy Castro

November 6, 1951 – February 14, 2012

It was now the beginning of a new year and already the middle of March. We were continuing to muddle through the grieving and healing process. After meeting the heart recipient's family and the liver recipient in person, I started wondering about the others and if we would ever meet them or if they had even wanted to hear from us. I went to the mailbox one day, and there it was - a letter from the kidney recipient's wife, dated January 1, 1991. It had taken the usual two-plus months for the LifeGift people to forward their letter on to us. I hurriedly opened the letter and read every detail.

We now had a first name, Jimmy. He and his family lived in Austin, he was thirty-nine years old, had been married sixteen years, and had a ten-year-old daughter. His wife began by writing they had received the letter I had sent through LifeGift, never expecting to hear from us, but it was a beautiful surprise, and they loved hearing about Jeff. She shared that Jimmy worked in the computer field, was active in the community through the National Kidney Foundation, local Chamber of Commerce, the city PTA and had been very active working with young people.

She enclosed a picture of Jimmy and their daughter, Noelle, taken just before Christmas on their first camping trip in three years. She ended that first letter by writing that they prayed for us, and we had a special place in their hearts. She said they would really love to hear from us again and asked for a picture of Jeff. What a treasure we had just received.

Of course, I called Dodie and told her of my surprise. She and I decided we should take a trip to Austin to do a little detective work with what little information I knew. A week later, she drove to Houston, picked me up and off we went to Austin. We started our investigation the afternoon we arrived. Knowing "Jimmy" was associated with the National Kidney Foundation, that is where we began. We took turns making calls and taking notes. I still have the scribbled notes we made after each call where we would find another piece of the puzzle. We were excited with the information we had gotten that first afternoon and began again the next morning.

By some miracle, we had his full name, where he worked, home phone number and address by that afternoon. I nervously dialed his phone number but got an answering machine, so I left a message telling him who I was, how I got his number, and where we were staying. We decided if we didn't hear back, I would write a note saying if he didn't want contact, we wouldn't bother them again. We would simply wish him a long and happy life. I would include the requested picture of Jeffrey, drop it at his office, knowing we had tried our best.

Shortly after making this decision and writing the note, the phone rang, and it was Jimmy. He was so excited and wanted us to meet him and his family that afternoon. They came over to our hotel, and as Dodie said, it was as if we had always known them. We took pictures, got lots of hugs, shared stories and left with grateful hearts. By the way, I also still have the note, written on Red Lion Hotels and Inns notepaper, dated March 26, 1991, that I had planned on leaving for Jimmy had we not heard from him.

This meeting began a long friendship, enhanced by many phone conversations with Jimmy and letters from his wife. The first letter we received from her was written a week after we met them. It started off, *"Dear Linda, Jerry, Dodie, and everyone else. It was so wonderful to meet you! I can't tell you how great it is to know who you are. Thanks so much for your effort, and I'm so glad that you had success in finding us."*

In her next letter she wrote, *"Linda, I have to thank you. When you visited us and we all spoke so frankly, our daughter was listening more closely than I thought. A lot of what you had reflected to us made an impression on her and really helped her deal with it. She had listened well and put her faith where it properly should be. A lesson well learned."* Jimmy told me after they received the picture of Jeffrey, their daughter decided she and Jeff looked alike. They did both have dark hair and brown eyes.

Jimmy shared with me that he had previously had a kidney transplant but had a reaction to one of the drugs, becoming extremely ill because of it. It had taken him two years to agree to be put back on the transplant list because of that experience. He also told me that Jeff's kidney was the closest match outside of being a family member that the doctors had ever seen. We were told this about other recipients as well. Amazing!

Early on, I got a call from Jimmy asking me one question. "Was Jeffrey stubborn?" Absolutely! He laughed and told me he really felt different and thought he was having a slight personality change. He said he had never been stubborn in his life up until now.

Another thing he shared with me was that he had never been a football fan and had not even watched a game until Jeffrey became part of him. One Saturday afternoon, he was changing TV channels and the Texas Tech football game was on. Before he realized it, he had sat there an hour watching it. He later told me he was really getting into these football games and couldn't believe he was enjoying them so much. I reassured him I knew Jeff would make a football fan out of him.

The calls and letters continued over the next twenty years until Jimmy became ill and his health remained on a downhill path. He lost his battle two years later. He led a normal, active life with Jeffrey's kidney, allowing him to see his daughter grow up, marry (her husband's name is Jeff), and have two granddaughters before he passed away. They were a blessing to us as we were to them. The following is the last letter we received from his wife telling us of his passing.

"My dear Atkins Family,

It is with a heavy heart that I write this brief letter. We lost our Jimmy on February 14th of this year after a lengthy illness.

By the very nature of events, our family had decided that this was the work of our Lord, calling Jimmy home. He will be missed, and he was well loved. He had a very good life. Not perfect, but he was indeed blessed. And in those blessings, we think of you all.

Jimmy was cared for where I work. He worked diligently in organ donor awareness. The Texas Organ Sharing Alliance is establishing a Tree of Life memorial in his name. I'm not quite sure of all the details, but it is indeed an honor to him, our family, and to you all-without whose love and generosity, his work would have never happened.

Thanks be to God for such blessings. Much love to all of you, Doreene."

Lung recipient – Robert (Rob)

Rob is the recipient with whom I had the least contact. We received the first of two letters from him written August 24, 1990. In the first letter, he shared with us that he was a forty-year-old investment banker, and he and his wife lived in North Dallas. He wrote that because of our generous decision to donate our son's organs, he was alive. Had he not received a lung when he did, he would have expired from a lung disease at age thirty-nine.

He went on to tell us that he had never smoked, nor did he work in an environment that is known to cause lung disease. He had become quite ill in a very short period. At the time of the first letter, he had recovered nicely, was swimming laps and back to other activities he had done before he became ill. His doctor told him he had received a good lung and had never transplanted a more perfect match.

I talked to Rob by phone only once after I found out his last name in April 1991. I knew he lived in North Dallas and decided to try to find him. In July, I was visiting my friend Deanna, and she told me the phone numbers in the telephone book that were for the North Dallas area. There were only three. I got a recording for the first number. The next two told me they were not who I was looking for. I later re-dialed the first one and explained to the man on the other end of the line whom I was looking for and he replied, "You got him."

We had a nice long chat, and he told me he was doing well. We received only one more letter from Rob, written December 15, 1991. This time he sent us a picture of himself and told us his transplant lung was rejecting, and he had been in the hospital. I was really surprised at this news. He said it was unclear at the time if he would be put back on the transplant list. We received word that in March 1992 he received a double lung transplant here in Houston. I kept up with his progress only for a short time before we lost touch.

Among other correspondence we received regarding recipients, was a thank-you letter from the Shriners Hospital Burn Unit in Galveston stating that a severely burned patient was also given the gift of life. They extended their sympathy and gratefulness that at the time of our loss, we had the greatness of spirit to consider the life of a person unknown to us. They related that there was no greater memorial to our son than to save the life of another human being. We appreciated their condolences and comforting note.

One other letter we received about specific recipients was from the Great Plains Lions Eye Bank, Inc. telling us of the two who received corneas. They were extremely grateful, and I was very happy for them because I think blindness is a terrible affliction. From the beginning, I did not want to meet them, and even now I can't explain why.

As I was gathering permission correspondence for this book, I was once again connected to the LifeGift organization. While communicating with the Family Service Coordinator, I was informed that the need for life saving transplants is more than five times greater than it was in 1990, increasing from 22,000 to over 113,000 on the waiting list. Roughly one person is added every ten minutes according to the United Network of Organ Sharing. What a precious and priceless gift life is.

Chapter 15

Letters Of Encouragement

As I said earlier, when I started writing about our experience, I read journals and correspondence Jeffrey had written mostly his last year in high school and first year of college. He was a gifted writer, and as I re-read them recently, I felt like these were almost heartfelt farewell letters to grandparents, family, and friends.

There were two letters in his college folder written to his best friend, Harold. The latest was written January 19, 1990, when Jeffrey told Harold what a great friend he had always been and how much fun he had being with him over the Christmas holidays. In this letter Jeffrey told Harold, *"I used to pray every day that you would come to Tech, so we could go to college together and share some more great memories, but now I think it's only right that you go to Liberty. Don't get me wrong, I still want you to come here, but I know that the Lord is calling you to Liberty and has a great plan for your life and we both know that what the Lord has in store for your life is always the correct way to go. You're lucky that you've realized what He wants you to do; I'm always wondering what He has in store for my life and what I should do. I've been praying that He'll open a door and show me what He has in store for me. Remember to pray for me so that an answer will come soon."* The Lord's plan for Jeff came six weeks later when He called him home to Heaven.

The Lord's plan for Harold Wayne Barron was to become a successful husband, father and pastor at Ridgecrest Baptist Church in Springfield, Missouri. I know Jeff is bursting with pride for his friend. So are we.

The Lord continued to bless us through the years with calls, cards and letters from our friends and visits from Jeff's friends. One Friday afternoon, our doorbell rang, and it was three of Jeffrey's friends. They were in town for their twentieth high school reunion and made a special effort to stop by and visit us before they went. Jerry and I were so touched by their thoughtfulness and thrilled to catch up on their lives.

One sweet and thoughtful gift was left at Jeffrey's grave in 2009. It was a gold-plated alumni lapel pin given to Jeff's cousin, Brian, in honor of his graduation from the School of Architecture at Texas Tech University. We were so touched by this precious gift. It is in safe-keeping until the appropriate time to return it. Thank you, Brian, for your unselfish act of kindness and for sharing your achievement with Jeff. Jeffrey would be so proud of your success.

Earlier, I wrote about Jeffrey buying a Bible for a young lady he was dating in the tenth grade. On March 10, 2009, we received a sweet note from her along with a copy of the note he had written to her in the Bible. In her new Bible, Jeffrey wrote, *"I may not always be everything you want, but I've given you the best gift I can. A new walk with God."* Jeff's friend said she still uses that Bible. She wrote, *"I truly believe God put Jeff in my life to strengthen my relationship with Jesus. He helped set a foundation of faith with me, which helped me to lead my husband to faith and now our children. I owe him so much for that."* What a priceless note and such a visual reminder of how the Lord uses each of us without us knowing why. Thank you, Sherry.

One more letter we received arrived twenty years after Jeff's death from another one of Jeffrey's friends whose dad was the one who cleaned up our courtyard while we were in Lubbock. It was a five-and a-half page letter telling us of two dreams he had of Jeffrey shortly after Jeff's death. He had wanted to tell us of his dreams years before but was afraid they would be too painful for us. He felt it was now time to share them.

In his first dream, he described a long staircase with a door at the top that he wanted to go through but couldn't. There was no person at the top. It wasn't a negative thing, instead a feeling of great comfort, but then he woke up.

A couple weeks later, he came home from college and was sleeping in his childhood bedroom again. Suddenly, he felt he was in a room that had two doorways with a light switch in the middle. He said Jeff was standing directly in front of him with the biggest smile he had ever seen. Jeff's hair was a little longer, frosted but still brown, and he looked the same. He was laughing and looking right at him with a huge smile. He said the giggle reminded him of the times when they were young, and Jeff would ask him to do his Jackie Gleason impressions from "Smokey and the Bandit" over and over while Jeffrey laughed hysterically. He said none of their other friends thought it was funny, but it was something Jeffrey requested a lot, and he obliged because he thought it was funny too.

In his dream, he stood in front of one door while Jeff stood in front of the other one, smiling and flipping the light switch on and off as only Jeff would do, yet the light never went off. His dream only lasted a few seconds, but in that short time, he saw Jeffrey happier than he had ever seen anyone in his life. He said when he woke up, he was overwhelmed with peace, joy, and happiness that he couldn't adequately explain.

The next morning, he shared his dream with his parents, his aunt, and later a couple of his friends, one being his future wife. A few years later, the book 90 Minutes in Heaven came out, and his wife told him he had to read it. He shared with us that there were so many similarities between what the book described and what he saw and felt in his dream of Jeffrey. He knew Jeff was in the presence of God, and he got to see a glimpse of Heaven that changed his life forever. Thank you, Steven, for sharing your dreams with us.

We have been asked several times over the years if we ever dreamed about Jeffrey or thought we saw him. The answer is yes. As you've guessed by now, Jeffrey loved his friends and always had lots of them. As silly as it sounds, Jerry started secretly worrying that Jeffrey would have no friends in Heaven. One day, as Jerry was in the shower, he plainly heard Jeff call his name, *Dad.* He flew out of the shower, grabbed a towel, and ran into the bedroom. There stood Jeff and a red-haired, freckled-faced boy about Jeff's age. Jeff clearly said, *"Dad, I want you to meet my friend ---." "---, this is my dad."* Jerry grabbed Jeff, hugging him and said there was no mistake that

Jeff hugged him back. He felt it. Jeffrey gave him a big smile, and then they were gone. Jerry said he ran all through the house calling Jeff's name, but to no avail. When he finally told me this story, he could remember every detail except the friend's name. He was grateful he had closure on this worry anyway.

I've only dreamed about Jeff two times. Each time he was walking toward me, smiling. He looked healthy and extremely happy. As I carefully looked him over, he walked straight through me and was gone. Both times he was neatly dressed in jeans and a shirt.

I was asked early on if I could, would I reverse the clock and have Jeffrey back. My answer was no, because I was sure he wouldn't want to come back. I believe with all my heart, once you experience Heaven, you would never want to leave.

Chapter 16

Epilogue

Several years ago, a Presbyterian minister, Reverend George A. Pera, preached on grief. The title of his sermon was "The Strange Gift." In his sermon, he related that *"Grief is life's lingering echo. It is the last long lingering tie that binds us to the one whom we no longer have. We can no longer touch them, see them, or feel them... but we can remember them, miss them, and grieve them. The grief hurts, but the gift the Lord has given us is the capacity to remember and feel grief rather than the power to forget and feel nothing."*

Looking back over the years since the Lord called Jeffrey home to Heaven, I'm still amazed at the many times that black cloud of grief overshadowed us. The Lord would compassionately blow it away, sending encouraging sunshine in many forms, even in a beautiful sunset or sunrise, showing His magnificent power.

I used to write scriptures on note paper and put them on the boys' bathroom counter and my kitchen counter, hoping it would be hidden in our hearts for encouragement. The scripture note that was there on March 10, 1990, was one of my favorite scriptures that I've clung to so often and know to be true. It is Lamentations 3:22-23. *"It's because of the Lord's mercies we are not consumed, His compassions never fail. They are new every morning; Great is His faithfulness."* Thank you, Lord, for your promises and your compassion.

As I reflect on the good times and bad, I'm reminded that our family has so much to be grateful for. We are so thankful for the nineteen years we were a family of four, and we have wonderful memories to look back on. We're grateful that the Lord knew beforehand that we would need Him to carry us through our darkest hours, and He did. We're so grateful we had loving families and dedicated friends to continuously stand firm with us during our time of great need.

Jerry and I are thankful that for the last twenty-one years, Jamey has been happily married to our sweet daughter-in-law whom we love very much. We are very proud of the husband and dad he has become and of his successful career with Chase Bank. He and Rachel have blessed us with two adorable granddaughters who are now fourteen and nine. We are fortunate to live close and be able to participate in their activities. The girls, Jessica and Amanda, talk about their Uncle Jeff as if they knew him personally because we've shared so many stories with them. He would have loved them dearly.

In the box of Jeff's school papers that I kept over the years, there's a booklet he made in elementary school titled "Fortunately and Unfortunately." He dedicated it to me with love. There is only one completed page, displaying a drawing of a boy. At the top is written, *"Fortunately I was born."* The rest of the pages are blank. This is exactly how I feel, fortunate and blessed. If before Jeff was born, the Lord had told me he would give me a son that I could only care for and love for nineteen years would I still want him, the answer would be absolutely! Just look at all the fun times we would have missed, the joy and excitement he generated for our family, and the lives he touched along the way.

With love and no regrets, until we meet again......Mom

Silent Rage

Silently I hung my head
With feelings of pain, rage & sorrow.
Asking myself why, and wondering
Is there a meaning to tomorrow?

My jaw was locked tight with hatred
Against a fate in which I had no control.
Jeff's body lay cold and motionless
Death having extracted its grissly toll.

They say "something" good will come from it,
Of this I have seen none.
I can only see the anger inside,
Knowing that I have lost a loved one.

On dark still nights I go and visit Jeff,
Remembering, wondering, laughing and crying.
Contemplating our lives that we shared,
Hating the memory of his dying.

Some nights, when Jeff and I are alone,
I scream out with Anger for none to hear.
So it remains my personal and silent Rage,
I then sit back and feel the many tears.

"Signed by" Stephen Burchett
In loving Memory of
Jeffrey Scott Atkins
Oct 26 '70 - Mar 10 '90

Chet, Stephen, Jeff & Jerry

My Friend

I have a friend, a precious friend
I have him like my brother.
Yes, his my friend, one of a kind
like him, there will never be another.

Jeff is his name, and I knew right from
the start.
That this friend of mine, one of a kind
Would have a special place deep
within my heart.

For many years we have laughed, we've
played, we've grown.
We shared so much, football, that little
black Mustang, a funny-face and even
our homes.

We had so many plans this special friend
of mine.
We did not know that God would call
him home so soon
My dearest friend, one of a kind!

Today we said God-by, but only for a season.
For you see we will meet again
We have a special reason!

His name is Jesus Christ.
He is our Lord + Saviour!
Because of him we have eternal life
We will both live forever!

So Jeff, my dearest friend,
please just keep in mind.
That I will always love you!
No one can take your place, you
are one of a kind!

for Harold
by
mom

101

Jeff & Harold at Graduation

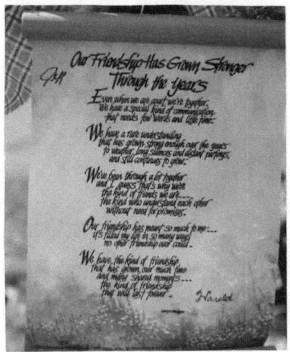

_Thank you
for all your love!!_

Mom,
I wanted to let you
know that I had a great
time last weekend. This card
explains it all. Thanks for
everything, & I love you.
Love Your Son.
Jeffrey Scott